THE
OVERNIGHT
GUIDE TO
PUBLIC SPEAKING

THE OVERNIGHT GUIDE TO PUBLIC SPEAKING

THE ED WOHLMUTH METHOD

By Ed Wohlmuth

RUNNING PRESS – PHILADELPHIA, PENNSYLVANIA

Printed in the United States of America.

Canadian representatives: General Publishing Co., Ltd.,
30 Lesmill Road, Don Mills, Ontario M3B 2T6.

International representatives: Worldwide Media Services, Inc.,
115 East Twenty-third Street, New York, New York 10010.

9 8 7 6 5 4 3 2 1
Digit on the right indicates the number of this printing.

Library of Congress Cataloging-in-Publication Number 89–43031

ISBN 0–89471–744–8

Cover design by Toby Schmidt.
Interior book design by Dennis Roberts.
Typography by COMMCOR Communications Corporation,
Philadelphia, Pennsylvania.

This book may be ordered by mail from the publisher.
Please add $2.50 for postage and handling for each copy.
But try your bookstore first!

Running Press Book Publishers
125 South Twenty-second Street
Philadelphia, Pennsylvania 19103

TABLE OF CONTENTS

Salesmen see their job as *selling*

The key to successful appearances

Doing your homework

TEN SURE-FIRE WAYS TO GIVE A LOUSY SPEECH

1. Come Ill-Prepared

After all, you're a busy person. They can't expect you to ignore all your important duties at the office just to prepare a little five-minute speech. Oh, can't they?

2. Waste Everyone's Time

Within 30 seconds, most audiences can tell whether a speaker means business. When the initial moments of the talk fail to give this evidence, even an important message can be buried in an avalanche of audience indifference.

3. Talk to Yourself

You don't care who the audience is or what they would

like to hear: what you have to say is *important*—at least to you. In the end, that'll be the sum total of your audience: you!

4. Talk to Your Boss

Who cares what all those nobodies think? The boss is out there, and *that's* who you're going to impress. Mention the name of your new product 18 times to show your enthusiasm. (Good! All those dealers will be sure to remember which product was represented by the speaker they hated the most.)

5. Use Opinions Instead of Facts

Cite some fancy names, and say they all endorse your position. After that, who cares what the facts are? Your opposition, that's who—and that's the next speaker on the schedule!

6. Ramble Away From Your Subject

That story good old Charlie told you yesterday was so funny you just *have* to work it into your speech. Trouble is, Charlie told that same story to half the people at yesterday's convention session—and the other half will wonder what it has to do with your topic.

7. Forget Your Objective

You love the sound of your voice so much, you've lost your main point amid a bouquet of sweet-sounding metaphors. You're not the only one who's lost!

8. Ignore the Setting

The headtable is crammed with speakers—seven of whom will follow your talk. Do you recognize this immediately, and win over the audience with a short-but-sweet address? No way! They gave you 15 minutes, and you're going to use every last second of it!

9. Ignore the Clock

You've made your point, but still you go on and on—unaware that the audience wants to move on to another topic (or adjourn the meeting). Result: the only thing they'll remember is that you didn't know when to quit.

10. Conclude Inconclusively

"Well, I guess that's all I have to say. . . ." You *guess?* If you don't *know,* you're *really* finished!

EVERYTHING YOU NEED TO KNOW ABOUT PUBLIC SPEAKING

. . . that can be put into a book on public speaking, is in this book.

That may sound like a tall order for a short book, but it really isn't. Everything that *needs* to be explained is explained. You'll even find subjects here that are seldom—if ever—covered in books two and three times the size. So how'd we keep this one so short? First, by leaving out all the things you *don't* need to know. That includes all the stories about "fabulous" speeches I gave here or there; this book is about you, not me. Second, by excluding all homework-type exercises. You and I both know you're not going to do them anyway.

Finally, you'll be surprised how much of this information you already know. Think of me as a professional guide giving you your first in-depth tour of your own hometown: you're familiar with all the landmarks, but just don't know their full significance. Once you understand what each point of interest really means, I can quickly move on to fresh territory. It's as simple as that.

How to Use This Book

If you'll be making a speech tomorrow, see "Instant Help," coming up next. Otherwise, your best bet is to read this book cover to cover. It will take one evening—at the most, two. That's the main reason it's been designed in this format. If you read it all from beginning to end, you'll find it's really *two* books in one. Here's why:

A straight-through reading will help you understand all the interrelated facets of public speaking: those that apply to every situation, and those that apply only in specific instances. Giving a speech at a luncheon involves the same basic rules as delivering the same speech at a dinner, but not the same *specifics*. Read everything—you never know when your phone may ring next and what type of presentation you'll be asked to make. Which brings us to book number 2.

The second book is a *reference* book, designed to be placed on a handy shelf for instant use the next time your phone does ring. Do they want you to speak at an evening meeting? Say you'll have to get back to them later, and don't say another word until you go back and reread that particular section.

You'll find this book especially helpful in the future if you take the time today to mark up sections and suggestions that zero in on your particular situation. Use a colored pencil to underline these items. I also hope you'll jot down anything of importance that comes to mind as you read each section. Use anything handy to make your notes—and place *everything* inside the covers of the book. In this way, you have only one item to locate when you go looking.

Assuming you still *have* the book! Please, don't loan it to anyone—not even a close friend. You'll end up calling eight or nine people (as I recently did), and none of them will have it. Not even the one who has it. No reflection on your friends; it's just that books seem to have feet of their own—and the smaller the book, the longer the walk. Your marked copy is *your* marked copy. Keep it that way.

INSTANT HELP

Are you faced with a public speaking task in the next 24 hours? Whether you're a first-time reader or simply reviewing this book as a refresher course, here are the sections to read when your time is limited:

1. The Subject of This Book is *You*
2. The Six Signals
3. A Speaker's Guide to Why and Where *[whichever sections apply]*
4. Putting Your Act Together
5. Drafting Your Speech
6. Preparing the Delivery

If time permits after you've completed the text of your speech, also read:

7. Preparing for the Podium
8. The Art of Introducing . . . and Being Introduced

ALL ABOUT ME

I said this book isn't about me, and it isn't. But to fully appreciate the information and suggestions it presents, you have to know a bit more about me than what appears on the book cover.

I'm now doing what I love most: writing and conducting seminars on a full-time basis. But before that, I spent almost two decades in the travel industry. With my father's early passing, I inherited a thriving company in the package-tour field. The job required extensive travel—in the United States and Canada—to give presentations on our products to groups of travel agents. Twice a year, I would have to "hit the road" with a contingent of colleagues for a series of cocktail parties, luncheons, and dinners throughout the continent.

In the beginning, I was scared stiff! I've always been comfortable communicating from behind a typewriter. But the thought of actually *talking* to people from behind a microphone was terrifying—all the more so because the company's success was at stake. I knew I had a problem—but business is business. I hit the road.

To my surprise (and delight) I found that my traveling companions had the same problem. I decided to give myself "on-the-job" training by closely observing everyone else's presentation deficiencies—as well as (to the best of my ability) my own.

Headtables have a lot of drawbacks, as I'll explain later, but they do offer speakers an unparalleled view of the *audience.* From my seat on the dais, I could see exactly what worked—and what didn't. I watched the heads of the audience, and I watched their eyes. And I kept an eye on the clock. Were people becoming bored because Bernie was running on too long about a particular feature of his hotel? I decided to shorten a similar portion of my own presentation. Was Ted disorienting the audience because the jumps in his talk were abrupt and unpredictable? I vowed to polish the continuity of my own talk, making each progression logical and easy to understand. And so on . . .

An unexpected and delightful bonus of those early years came in the person of storyteller Myron Cohen. Myron, who was to be featured along with other stars in our entertainment package, traveled with us to sixteen cities and wowed each and every audience—luncheon, dinner, whatever. Not only did he prove to be a sensational traveling companion (swallowing a mouthful of scrambled eggs just as Myron hit one of his breakfast-table punch lines became one of life's more interesting challenges), but I learned an enormous amount of show business savvy from him in a short amount of time. And I discovered that what my colleagues, and I were doing was *also* show business.

Every tip, technique, and suggestion you are going to read in these pages has its origin back in those years on the road, and in speeches and presentations I've made—or watched others make—before almost every type of audience. Over the years I've also been deeply involved in planning meetings and seminars—another source of this book's information. I've worked with every conceivable type of hotel function and ballroom facility: the places where the great majority of public speaking tasks are performed. I've learned that the time of day, the type of function, the food, the booze, the service, and countless other items all help determine the success or failure of a presentation. I know what audiences expect of speakers and how they form those expectations. Most of all,

I know that the methods I teach *work*. Some are deceptively simple, but they *do* make a difference.

THE SUBJECT OF THIS BOOK IS YOU

Who are you? I don't know. I don't know your age, your sex, your situation in life. Believe it or not, that's a plus—because I can't take anything about you for granted. And I won't; there's help here for *everyone*.

The amount of help you get out of this book, however, is up to you. Why do you want to improve your public speaking—for professional reasons, social acceptance, or both? How hard are you willing to work, and how many things are you willing to change, in order to achieve that goal? Almost all of the suggestions in this book can be implemented right away—but every one requires some action or behavior modification on your part. Many will produce almost immediate results, but others will take some time. I hope you're willing to devote the time, but even if you're not, read on—you may find yourself changing your mind in a few minutes.

Let's talk for a few seconds about your personality. Are you shy? Uncomfortable in crowds? Nothing builds confidence like hearing applause from an appreciative audience. I know many people who are shy and unhappy in crowds, and who are *also* dynamite speakers. The key is lack of intimidation. They know what they're doing and aren't scared stiff by the prospect of speaking before a group. (Not any more!)

Take note, however, that their *basic* personalities have remained the same. If you're basically a shy, soft-spoken person, *The Overnight Guide* won't transform you into an assertive, bouncy individual. The person at the microphone will always be the basic *you*. That's a plus, because it's exactly what the audience wants, not some phoney-baloney person you've concocted just for the occasion. That's what this book is all about: helping you to say what *you* want to say, in your style, and in your words.

Hardly anyone explains this, but there are *two* cornerstones to successful public speaking—one that can be taught, and one that can't. The one that can be taught—and is the key to everything in this book—in *preparedness*. The one that can't be—and is an important element to your over-all success—is your ego: you, as you see yourself as a think-ing, feeling, functioning individual. How do you see yourself in relation to other people? Do you consider yourself more knowledgeable and/or successful than others, less so, or pretty much on an even keel? Do other people intimidate you? If so, how?

Maybe you can answer those questions honestly, and maybe you can't. Americans place a great deal of stock—some people think far too much—in our job titles, or lack of same. If you're a travel agent and think that travel agents are somehow outclassed by airline employees, you're going to have one hell of a time trying to talk to a group of airline employees on *any* subject. If the reverse is true, and you think that travel agents are superior, you're still going to have a problem. The problem is the mismatch, no matter which side it falls on. Audiences, as you're going to see, have egos, too.

A true story: Some years back, I found myself in an air-plane seat next to a well-dressed executive who was poring over what looked like some company's annual report—one of those documents with a plastic cover and a spiral binder. I was busy with work of my own, and we didn't exchange any words until lunch arrived; then I found him eager to talk, in that strange way nervous people always are. He was on his way to a convention, where he had to give a major address that very evening. The speech—his speech—was the item in the plastic binder. It had been written by the senior member of his public relations department ("Great writer, you should see some of his stuff . . ."), and the executive was reading it through for the first time on that flight! "No problem," he said, "I'll be ready for 'em."

Do you wonder, as I did, how " 'em" received that speech? By chance, I knew someone who was scheduled to attend that convention. A week later, I made a point of calling her to ask if she had attended that session and heard that particular speech. She had indeed. How was it?

"You know," she replied. "The usual corporate bullshit!"

Imagine that you and I were sitting next to each other in the audience that night. Just before the executive is introduced, I whisper to you that his speech was really written by some guy in the P.R. department. Do you feel slighted? Angry that the executive didn't care enough about the people in the audience to write his own damn speech? That's *your* ego. *His* ego told him he could do it and get away with it, and that you wouldn't know the difference. And there's the mismatch.

However the mismatch occurs, audiences *do* know, and they will respond with emotions that run from pity to outright anger. When these emotions are present, your message will *not* get through—which brings us back to you.

As you've probably figured out already, the most common ego mismatch happens when the speaker places his or her ego *below* that of the audience—for that moment, anyway. In the speaker's mind, the audience is judge, jury, and executioner. "How did you do?" "God! They killed me!" That answer is often closer to the truth—as seen in the mind of the speaker—than anyone suspects.

Audiences do not kill. In fact, they don't even like to *disapprove!* Audiences want to *applaud;* they want to affirm a great performance. Why? Because in doing so, they affirm their own wisdom in coming to the event in the first place. People don't like to think of themselves as suckers. ("I should have known better than to go to that luncheon!")

Believe me, the audience is on *your* side. They want you to succeed. Do *you* want to succeed? Good, then you and the audience are on the *same* ego level. Only when you permit some other factor to intrude—an inferior or superior work-role ego, for example—does a true mismatch occur. I can't help you with that problem (other than to suggest some professional counseling if the problem is really serious). But if you recognize that a problem may exist, you are well on your way to finding a solution. I hope so. And I hope you'll mark this section and reread it every time you're faced with a public speaking opportunity.

So now you know why that small disclaimer is in the opening sentence of the book. Everything you need to know about public speaking, *that can be put into a book on public speaking,* is in this book. Nothing more. And hopefully nothing less.

Johnny, Phil, Merv & Mark

Does the thought of speaking before a group scare the living daylights out of you? You have tons of company. Recent public opinion polls show that among people from virtually all walks of life, fear of public speaking is now incredibly common—ranking right up there with "fear of the unknown," the traditional all-time leader.

Interestingly, this fear has emerged on a national level in an era when the "talk show" has also emerged as a feature of daily life. I don't think that's merely a coincidence.

The largest single pool of potential guests for these shows are the authors of new books. But guests are also drawn from the professions, business, industry, agriculture, the arts, you name it. "Just plain people" telling stories of life's various adventures are also a common feature, particularly on local talk shows. But it's the network and syndicated shows, with their huge national audiences, that can be the strongest negative influence on a beginner's confidence. The Chicago-based *Donahue,* considered the trendsetter on discussions of "hot" topics (particularly for women), can be especially intimidating to the novice speaker because it features not only fast-paced exchanges between host Phil Donahue and his guests but also audience and phone-in participation. Even the show-business-oriented *Merv Griffin Show,* with its relaxed, "tell-us-everything" atmosphere, contributes to the problem. Thus it's easy to assume that everyone in the country is ready to settle in before microphones and cameras at a moment's notice, and only *you* are scared bananas by the thought.

Nothing could be further from the truth.

The process of picking guests is *highly* selective. Hidden behind all this local and national on-the-air activity are the professional production staffs who screen potential guests (even show-business personalities), insuring that everyone who makes it before cameras and microphones really does have something to say, and can say it effectively. Even the phone-in shows can be deceptive: many route incoming calls to one or more screening producers before allowing the callers anywhere near the host.

But nowhere are appearances more deceptive than with Johnny Carson, the role model against whom millions of would-be speakers judge themselves. And here, the deception works in an entirely different direction.

Since its inception over two decades ago, *The Tonight Show Starring Johnny Carson* (that's its official title) has been built around its host's rare gift for knowing precisely what will, or will not, "play" at any given moment—and a highly deceptive talent for getting positive results out of bad jokes and mishaps, by creating laughter at his own expense. (Jack Benny, an early Carson influence, also had this gift—and was also underestimated by some of the audience.) Thus, the more-than-occasional "clinker" in the monologue, or the zoo animal that suddenly stains an expensive new sportscoat—features that observers say are carefully orchestrated into the show—provide just such opportunities.

Supporting all of this is a staff of almost 200 production, technical, and support personnel who provide the show with its unique combination of show business glitter and spontaneous activity—while controlling both to the greatest degree possible. Prospective guests are carefully screened and interviewed, and notes on each are prepared well in advance of air time. In this way, the star always knows where he is going—or has a backup position ready in the event a spontaneous discussion takes a wrong turn—preparations that *all* speakers in informal situations would be extremely wise to emulate, even if they can't emulate the style of the man himself.

And no one can. Johnny Carson is unique among the performers of our era; making the most difficult of all tasks—the constant, night-after-night, solid performance—look incredibly easy.

But Carson isn't the only "look-how-easy-it-is" role model being used these days. The daily broadcast listings also provide David Hartman, Joan Lunden, and their colleagues on *Good Morning America;* Bryant Gumbel and company of *Today* (all of whom are hard at work preparing and rehearsing at hours the rest of us would consider obscene); Robert MacNeil and Jim Lehrer on public television's *MacNeil/Lehrer Report;* Susan Stamberg and associates on National Public Radio's *All Things Considered;* plus all of the aforementioned talk-show hosts, and every local and national newscaster, sports commentator, and weather forecaster—especially those using the "happy talk" format of seemingly impromptu banter between news stories.

It's interesting to note that all of these local and national personalities are in high demand on the so-called rubber-chicken circuit—the plethora of banquets held from one end of the country to the other. But as almost every program chairman will attest, not all are strong performers at the podium. Working on the air is far different from speaking to a live audience—as many of the personalities themselves will gladly admit.

On the air, however, everything functions with precision and grace—the common denominators being hard work, a talent for making it look easy, and visible or hidden support systems of notes, cue cards, and prompting devices.

All of which makes it quite remarkable when a performer comes along who works largely without support devices. And for the past seven years, just such a *tour de force* has been taking place on public television, and influencing a large, national audience. From the moment on his bi-monthly PBS special when the announcer crows, "And now, *live* from Buffalo. . ." to the sign-off twenty-eight minutes later, political humorist Mark Russell performs his unique brand of satirical songs and topical humor entirely without the benefit of a safety net. No cue cards, no nothing. Live—on national TV.

Once again, it all looks deceptively easy. It isn't. I think you'll find what *really* happens very instructive, and I'm indebted to Mark for sharing his method of preparation with us.

The starting point on this short journey is a gift for comedy, honed to a razor-fine edge over a twenty-year career on the banquet and campus concert circuit (he now performs

about 100 of these concerts a year, usually to packed houses)
and until recently, as star-in-residence at Washington's
Shoreham Hotel, where he was a great favorite of the very
politicians he uses as foils. Here's Mark:

> *The layman thinks of what I do as simply
> memorizing a half-hour speech with songs thrown
> in, but it's much more complex than that. My
> material is a crazy quilt of little portions—little
> hunks memorized by subject—that can be rear-
> ranged or discarded depending on what's timely,
> what's new, and what's working.*
>
> *I start preparing for each special on the morning
> after the last one, which gives me about seven or
> eight weeks of time. I write new material every
> morning—and I put it on 3-by-5 cards—and then I
> tape it into a cassette recorder. Each morning I add
> to the tape—a little bit more each time—and after
> two weeks, I've got enough to try that little hunk on
> stage at one of my concerts. I carefully slip it in
> between pieces of my regular material to see how
> the audience will react. I do that with each little
> portion I add.*
>
> *Each TV special has about four songs, and the
> trick is to get them written early. It takes a long time
> to practice a song until you're delivering it properly.
> So I also work on finishing the songs as quickly as
> I can.*
>
> *About two weeks before the special, I have
> enough new material for the complete twenty-eight
> minutes—and also a completely timed tape that
> allows for the eight seconds or so of applause after
> each song, plus a small amount of space at the top
> of the show for anything important that's happened
> that day. And I'm ready to try the whole thing out
> on stage, but still not in the order that it's going to*

be seen on TV—each hunk still has to be slipped in and out of my regular material. But it gives me enough time to throw something out if it isn't working.

By the day before the show, everything's in place and we have a timed rehearsal at the theater [The Katharine Cornell Theatre at the State University of New York at Buffalo] with a small audience of stage crew and theater personnel. Then, on the day of the broadcast, we do it again—about two hours before air time, with all the cameras working. Then the audience comes in, and we go live, and that's the first time anyone's seen that particular twenty-eight minutes of material performed in that order. . .

As you can see, the secret to Mark's ability to work without a safety net has three parts: preparation, rehearsal, and enough time to do both properly. You may not have seven weeks or even seven days, but you can take advantage of this proven method. All it takes is the will to succeed.

THE VIEW FROM THE AUDIENCE

It makes no sense to talk about the details of public speaking until we first examine the nature of the audience. Everything in public speaking revolves—or *should* revolve—around this collective body. Yet the nature of audiences is widely misunderstood—by speakers, by audience members, and even by some professional performers. (The ones who make it to the top and stay there know audiences better than anyone on the planet.)

We'll examine the different types of audiences a little later. First, let's see what all *voluntary* gatherings of people have in common.

Majority Rules!

The first common trait of all audiences is simple: the majority *rules!* You've seen this phenomenon at work many times, but a simple exercise will prove the point. Next time a top-rated comedy is playing at a first-run movie theater, walk in halfway through the 5 P.M. dinner-time show. Then keep your seat for the 7 P.M. show, which should be far more crowded. What you will observe, and may have observed before, is that while larger audiences generate great volumes of laughter, a smaller audience may hardly laugh at all. How come? Because many people feel self-conscious about laughing out loud in a half-empty theater, and the majority *always* rules.

Attend a symphony concert, and you'll see the rule at work in another way. Most people feel guilty about coughing while the music is being performed and try to stifle this reflex to conform to the audience majority—who are, of course, stone silent. But allow six or seven people to cough during one of the breaks, and suddenly it may seem that half the audience is coughing!

Audiences feed on themselves. Most are composed of individuals of widely varying backgrounds, tastes, and personal circumstances, but when it comes to *that* particular collective body, the behavior and attitude of the majority will rule the entire room. Laughter reinforces laughter; silence reinforces silence. It's why getting someone to ask that first question—if you want the audience to ask questions—is so difficult.

Understand this rule, and you'll immediately know how to treat the person who's asleep in the third row—the most common problem faced by all speakers, novice and expert alike. You'd be surprised how many experienced speakers are really flustered when this occurs—only because they do not understand the true nature of audiences. In an attentive audience, the sleeper is *abnormal*, someone who is bucking convention because there's a strong *individual* reason to do so. It might be boredom, but it's far more likely that the person just *needs* sleep. Ignore the snoozer—and the person in the sixth row who looks bored to tears. If you can win the *majority* of your audience, you've won the day!

THE OUTSIDE ALWAYS COMES IN

An audience does not exist in a vacuum. It is the collective product of everything that has happened to each person—individually and as a member of the group—long before you set foot on the rostrum. Outside influences always come inside the meeting room. They may be headlines in the morning paper, a lousy breakfast served by the convention caterer, or a nephew who has suddenly died. Nor do these influences necessarily have to be negative: the stock market could be up fifty points!

Outside influences on audiences have become very strong. Commercials are an enormous factor, but they also include every newspaper, TV or radio show, billboard, trade publication, convention announcement, and transit ad to which the audience has been exposed—collectively or as individuals. That's a huge mass of information, much of it arriving in high-impact, visual formats. No wonder there's an increasing tendency for audiences to "tune out" and daydream—another aspect of modern life that people bring into the meeting room from outside. Here again, the rule is

simple: an audience will daydream at the slightest opportunity and will not return to reality without a strong incentive. Once erected, a daydream is a formidable barrier.

GREAT EXPECTATIONS

It would be natural to assume that an audience's level of
expectation is colored by the vast number of bad speeches
they're exposed to. That used to be the case, but today the
expectation level is very high—and continues to rise.

More than any other single factor, the emergence of the
seminar business as a full-fledged industry has upgraded the
public-speaking expectation level of all audiences. Once the
exclusive province of the business community, seminars are
now offered in virtually every walk of life, and the men and
women at the top levels of the business today are unexcelled
at audience motivation. Full-time professionals have a unique
advantage: When you do the same thing day after day, you
can see exactly what works, and doesn't work, with a wide
range of audiences—and get mighty good at your craft.

That's your competition—and don't make the mistake of
thinking that the working audience is the only group to
which it applies. Social audiences almost always consist of
one half or more working individuals—particularly men and
women from the world of business—who bring their
seminar-generated expectations right along. Remember, no
audience exists in a vacuum, and the majority *always* rules.

For experienced speakers, the lesson here is obvious: what
"got by" in the past will no longer work. Audiences *do* want
you to succeed; but the quality of performance necessary for
success is higher than ever before.

Ears Have Lousy Memories

For some oddball reason no one really understands, the ear triggers a very limited memory effect in the brain. It's why people shopping for hi-fi loudspeakers become so bewildered and annoyed with what should be a pleasant task: it's almost impossible to compare models heard in different stores—and at different times. Auditory memory is limited, and this phenomenon directly affects an audience's ability to *remember* what it hears during the course of *any* oral presentation. A great deal of the advice contained in this book is based on that single factor.

To add yet a further complication, it's now well established that the brain can process information about four to five times faster than the normal rate of speech. A good example is the party-goer who can listen to a joke and think of one to tell at the same time, and almost everyone's capable of that.

So what you face in *any* audience is a group of people with overtaxed memories and undertaxed thinking abilities. Now you see why daydreaming is so tempting: it's far easier to let the imagination play with that excess brain power than to try to stuff words and ideas into an uncooperative retention system.

Every Audience Has an Ego

Student audiences have changed dramatically over the past four decades. In the '50s, it was almost unthinkable for students to challenge a lecturing professor; today, it's routine. "OK, that's what you *say* happens—now *prove* it!" The collective ego of the college classroom says that the students are entitled to this information and are *not* required to give the professor the benefit of the doubt.

Every audience has a collective ego that sets the standard for what the group believes it's entitled to—and what it, in turn, is required to give the speaker. Yet the collective ego in the most frequently overlooked factor in explaining the nature of audiences. It is determined by a number of factors, most of which are easily identified. A professional audience, for example, has a totally different ego than a sales audience. An audience attending "by invitation only" has different characteristics than a "come-one-come-all" audience. And an audience sharing the same occupation is far different from one where many diverse occupations are represented. For now, don't worry about *how* they're different; just know that each has its own distinct ego.

30-Second Wonder

The 30-second television commercial is really a little playlet: it has an introduction, a plot exposition, and a finale. Since it attacks the senses on two levels, visual and auditory, it has a high degree of impact; and since it also addresses the perceived needs for safety, comfort, acceptability, recreation, and status, it can create an emotional response on both conscious and subconscious levels. In other words, people go out and buy things!

But the 30-second commercial has done a lot more to American life than just sell us billions of dollars' worth of goods and services. It has shortened everyone's attention span and made us very impatient with inefficient forms of communication. Whatever else it is, the 30-second spot is *very* efficient. It will not only tell you how others have benefited from the product and why you should have it, but also how much it costs and where you can get it. All in 30 seconds. No wonder audiences get furious with speakers who take a half hour—the equivalent of *sixty* TV commercials—to deliver what amounts to a single sales pitch.

When I explain this factor to my seminar groups, the usual reaction is amusement and disbelief: "Aw, who watches that garbage?" is a pretty standard comment. But, I argue, it isn't *all* garbage. Give me some companies who have had really outstanding commercials in the past few years.

"Federal Express!" OK . . .

"Miller Lite!" Right . . .

"Polaroid!" All right . . .

By the time I'm ready to acknowledge the fourth raised hand, the room is filled with laughter—and sometimes applause—and I've made my point: we *all* watch that garbage, and we watch it a *lot*. TV commercials are a very pervasive influence on all audiences; and, lest you think they're the only tube-delivered shorteners of the American attention span, the average time network newscasts allot to each news story is now under two minutes, and growing shorter.

All of us want our information in fast, compact, digestible units. That's why you may never again let yourself give a long-winded talk. It's definitely why I wouldn't let this become a long-winded book.

The Six Signals All Audiences Want to Hear

ONE: I will *not* waste your time.

TWO: I know who *you* are.

THREE: I am well *organized*.

FOUR: I *know* my subject.

FIVE: Here is my most *important* point.

SIX: I am *finished*.

THE SIX SIGNALS

Here's the most important information in this book, and the cornerstone of my public speaking method.

All audiences want to hear the Six Signals. They want to hear them from every speaker. They want to hear them regardless of the length of your talk, or its topic. Most of the signals do not have to be given directly—they can be implied by your words. But you *must* give them.

As you read through each explanation, you'll recognize many points we've already covered returning in more concrete forms—and you'll see why knowing the nature of your audience is crucial to everything in public speaking.

Here are the signals:

SIGNAL NUMBER ONE: "I WILL *NOT* WASTE YOUR TIME"

Time has become our most precious commodity. There simply aren't enough hours in the day to do all the things we want to do; and we take far more time deciding what to do with our time than we do deciding what to do with our money. That's a fact. Did you make any money decisions in the past hour? How about time decisions? What else did you consider doing before you decided to read this book?

As with all decisions, we want our time decisions validated; that is, we want to be told (by ourselves or someone else) that we've made the right choice. When we learn otherwise, we can get very angry.

Audiences get angry when they sense that their time is being wasted. And anger is such a powerful emotion that it can overrule any other motives they have for paying attention.

The collective ego of the audience—any audience—says that the group is entitled to spend its time in a meaningful manner. When a speaker validates this feeling, the audience feels good about itself (because it has made the right choice in being there) and it feels good about the speaker.

You must give the "I will not waste your time" signal very early—preferably in the first 10 seconds of your remarks. Here's an example:

> *Thank you, Tim, for that gracious introduction, and good morning everyone. I'd like to begin* [signal] *my brief remarks* [reinforcing signal] *by asking all of you to consider where we'd be today without modern, computerized banking.*

See how easy it is? The speaker has given the signal quickly and gone on to the real business at hand—and to a very attentive (and appreciative) audience.

Here's another example—this time by a speaker who's making a banquet introduction:

> *Good evening. I know you're all anxious* [signal] *to hear from our guest speaker tonight, so I'll just tell you one or two things* [reinforcing signal] *I don't think you know about him.*

Note that the initial signal is generally followed by a reinforcing signal so that the audience can't possibly mistake your meaning. But be careful not to promise the audience something you can't deliver; use the word "brief" only if that's what it's really going to be. A longer talk is not necessarily a time waster, and you may have good reason for needing more time. But never try to fool the audience on this point. They will begin listening for a concluding statement long before you're ready to give one, and will stop listening to what you're *actually* saying.

Also avoid statements like, "In the few minutes I have available. . ." While this sort of message may sound like an excellent signal, it also suggests a possible restriction. The audience can easily interpret the statement as, "I don't have enough time to do a proper job," or, "You're not going to get all the information you're entitled to." If this is really the case, it's your fault. You should have never taken on that particular speaking assignment—a point we'll cover again later in the book.

I'm frequently asked whether jokes and stories are considered time-wasters; especially as it was once fashionable to teach public-speaking students that a good opening joke can "loosen up" an audience. For reasons that I'll explain later, joke telling is extremely dangerous. I usually advise against it. But there are occasions when a *true* incident, unknown to the audience, makes an excellent opener. Here's an example of the signal coupled with the story introduction:

> *As you know, my subject this morning is fire prevention. In a few seconds* [signal], *I'm going to give you the three cornerstones of good fire safety* [reinforcing signal]. *But first, I'd like to tell you a true story about a boy, a dog, and a box of matches . . .*

I can't imagine anyone in the audience not wanting to hear that story. The important thing is that it's *relevant to the speaker's topic.*

Everything in your talk must be relevant. You cannot give the "I will not waste your time" signal at the beginning of your speech and then wander off to uncharted waters—if you do, your audience will consider you untruthful. This requires you to be a good editor, eliminating anything in your talk that isn't right on the mark. If you take great pains to do so, your effort will be amply rewarded.

Finally, the first signal is of little value standing on its own. Each of the signals is interrelated to all the others. The six signals are a *unit* and must be used as such.

SIGNAL NUMBER TWO: "I KNOW WHO *YOU* ARE"

Nothing puts an audience into a speaker's pocket better than a speech that zeroes in on their specific needs. When you're talking directly to their selfish interests, people tend to "put their ears on"—in the wonderful truckers' language of CB radio.

Not only must you know your audience, you must *tell* them so. And once again, it should be done as early in your talk as possible. Here's the third sentence of our example speech on computerized banking:

> At First Widget Bank, we have many retail merchant clients [signal] who, like you [reinforcing signal], have severe cash-flow problems."

That's right on the mark for a group of local shopkeepers. It says that the speaker not only knows the audience members but is aware of one of their more serious problems. It also suggests that a solution will be offered—which heightens attention even more.

"Fine," you may say, "but what if I'm talking to a general

audience without specific or identifiable needs?" My answer is that every audience possesses a common ground somewhere. Listen, for example, to the editor of a women's fashion magazine talking to a predominantly male lodge audience:

> *I know you're all not sitting there breathless* [signal], *waiting for the latest fashion news from Paris or New York. But you might like to know how much time the women in your lives* [reinforcing signal] *will probably be spending in the stores this fall—and what they will look like when they emerge* . . .

Of course, our example presumes that the editor really has some hot news to impart—skirt lengths going back down to the floor, for instance. If not, the speaking invitation probably should have been declined. (No one wants to listen for 15 minutes only to discover that nothing's changing.)

By the same token, audiences want you to acknowledge how much they *already* know—an equally important part of the signal. Professional audiences, for instance, want you to credit them with a certain level of expertise in their chosen field, or acknowledge that they have reached a certain level of social accomplishment —a thing that show business veterans call "covet," which roughly translates to, "Give me the respect/attention/love I am due."

Thus, a builder who tries to explain an age-old construction process to a group of architects is in for big trouble—even if several members of the audience really *aren't* familiar with the technique. And a group of surgeons doesn't want to have its mutual nose rubbed in the questionable ethics of a few physicians. The collective ego of the audience says they are entitled to better treatment, and that you, the speaker, should know it.

I have seen this rule violated many times, with results ranging from complete audience indifference to the speaker, all the way up (down is more accurate) to catcalls and boos. And I have a very vivid memory of a former colleague who *assumed* that the name of the organization he was invited to address gave him all he needed to know. It didn't. It was deceptive, and he ended up giving a speech that left the audience totally bewildered—and the speaker very red in the face. (Never assume that the National Association of Bridge Specialists are a bunch of construction engineers. They might really be *dentists!)*

You *must* know your audience. If you're not an insider, try to find out everything there is to know about the group and tailor your remarks accordingly. If that isn't worth doing, the talk isn't worth giving. If it is worth doing, do it and give the signal.

Signal Number Three: "I Am Well *Organized*"

Reading a book is far different from listening to a speech. As a reader, you maintain absolute control over the flow of information, and anything not understood on first reading can be returned to for review—again and again, if you like. As an audience member, however, you get only one bite at the apple: if you don't understand the information *instantly,* it is of little or no value. That should be self-evident to all speakers, but unfortunately it isn't.

As you now know, there are severe restrictions on the ability to remember information arriving in oral form. This places a burden on the speaker to *organize* the message into a clear, easily-understood unit—so that the audience's retention capabilities will not be taxed beyond their limits. But on top of that, the audience must be *told* that the speech is organized—and, if possible, *how*.

You've already seen an example: our fire-prevention introduction told the audience that three major points were coming up. This gives the listener a chance to organize the listening process, to open up three cubbyholes in the memory banks for incoming material.

Here's some more of our computerized banking speech:

> *There are two sides* [signal] *to the cash-flow problem—ours and yours—and I want to spend a few moments discussing each with you before turning to a possible solution* [signal] *for both of us.*

Note how the banker is setting up the audience: the merchants have now been told that there are going to be *two* discussions of problems, followed by a single proposed solution. Note also how Signal Number One ("few moments") and Signal Number Two ("ours and yours") are woven into the same statement.

Here's the same principle woven into a talk in a much lighter vein. The speaker is a baseball manager:

> *I've been asked many times about the eccentricities of our star pitcher, Jigs O'Daferty. There are hundreds of stories I could tell you about Jigs; but since you're all connected with the grocery field, I've chosen three stories—one involving a banana, another a box of cereal, and a third about a head of lettuce.*

I'd like to hear those stories myself. The point is, the manager has *organized* his talk and has indicated this to his audience. Signal Number Two is pretty self-evident—having chosen stories just for them, the baseball manager gives the grocery store operators a sense of identity and importance. Signal Number One is represented by the statement that hundreds of possible stories on Jigs are on tap—of which three have been selected.

Later, we'll discuss the preparation of your talk in detail, but there's one point that must be made here. Whether you read your speech from a full text, or deliver it from notes, it must contain *short, clear,* logical statements. And each statement must open the door for the one to follow. In this way, you lead the listener through your presentation, step by step. Avoid compound sentences, multiple subjects, parenthetical phrases, qualifications, foreign words and expressions, and anything else that might shake the listener off the track of what you really mean. On paper, the results may look a little stilted—and perhaps they do require some smoothing out. But remember, reading it and listening to it are two *different* things. I can't emphasize that enough.

SIGNAL NUMBER FOUR: "I *KNOW* MY SUBJECT"

We live in the Great Age of Specialization. Just look at the want ads in *The Wall Street Journal:* Wanted: Securities Attorney. Wanted: Corporate Vice President, Strategic Planning. Wanted: Chemical Engineering Writer.

It's natural, therefore, that audiences want speakers who possess levels of expertise that qualify them to talk with authority. But even when this happy match-up occurs between speaker and topic, the audience must be *told* that it exists, or they won't put the message in maximum focus. Part of this burden falls on the speaker's introduction, but the entire *responsibility* falls squarely on the speaker.

Introductions are covered later in the book. Here, the important point is that an introduction cannot stand on its own; it must be reinforced by the words of the talk. Here are the signals in the next section of our computerized-banking speech:

> *On our side of the cash-flow problem, we have the responsibility to clear your deposited checks as quickly as modern technology will allow—and that's where my job comes in. The programs our computer uses to do this are my personal* [signal] *responsibility. This means that I must be on constant guard to insure* [reinforcing signal] *that our electronic capabilities are being properly matched to your needs.*

Note what has *not* been said. There is no indication that the banker has all the magic answers; only that the responsibility falls personally on the speaker to match the bank's computer programs with the merchants' needs. The speaker has given the signal without appearing pompous or overbearing—another vital point to remember.

The old saw, "all of us are ignorant, about different things," is more apt than ever. Never forget that your audience, too, represents a high level of expertise—on many diverse subjects. Next week *you* might be sitting out there while one of *them* is at the podium. What type of signal would give *you* positive feelings about the speaker?

On the other hand, you must be careful not to underqualify yourself. Here's a professional press photographer talking to a group of advanced amateurs. Watch how camera jargon and techniques known to the group are carefully woven into the signals:

My topic this evening is how to maintain proper
depth-of-field while composing pictures in grab-shot
situations. As all of us know [signal], *zoom lenses,*
with their restricted maximum apertures, are not
ideal for shooting in low-light situations. And in my
line of work [reinforcing signal], *you never know*
when just such a situation will suddenly arise . . .

The press photographer could have easily said, "We don't
use zoom lenses at the newspaper," but that would not have
qualified the speaker in the eyes of the audience. The trick
is to use words that will appeal to the audience on its own
level (thus, again, reinforcing their sense of identity and importance) while establishing your own credentials on a slightly higher level.

But you *do* have to know what you're talking about.
Watergate and J.R. Ewing have made us all skeptical of our
fellow human beings—and the advertising world is filled with
a lot of hype that, unfortunately, isn't matched by product
performance. The burden of proof is always on you.

Business executives are especially prone to this problem
because many assume their job titles automatically confer
a level of expertise that others should acknowledge. Not only
is this untrue, but audiences can frequently be left wonder-
ing why the executive's services are needed at all. Here's a
corporate vice-president who chose an amusing way to hit
that problem head-on. The audience is a convention in
another field:

I have three points to cover this morning [organ-
ization signal], *and each will take about five minutes*
[time signal]. *But first, let me take a few seconds* [rein-
forced time signal] *to tell you about a phone call I*
received last week from our director of communi-

cations. "Charlie," he said, "we'd like to feature your department in the next issue of our company magazine." "Great," I said, "I'll look forward to getting my copy." "OK," said the director, "but that's not why I'm calling. Just what is it you guys do up there?"

The cleverness of this device (and that's what it is; the incident never happened) is that it lets the executive explain his function without casting the audience's knowledge level in a negative light—after all, there are people in his own company who don't know his function. Many other devices can be used with similar ends.

One frequently used device in fund-raising talks is the work-in-progress description. Thus the audience is given an *immediate* goal it can contribute toward. Here's the research director of a medical foundation who's using the device in this way—and also for the purpose of establishing credentials:

> *I know you'll all be excited to learn that we're nearing a breakthrough on this dread disease. Given your continued support, it's just a matter of time. In particular, the work of Dr. Kellar, at our Denver facility, is showing great promise. The daily reports that cross my desk are filled with important facts that we're passing along to our colleagues in the drug field . . .*

Note how the speaker casts the audience in a humanitarian light by *assuming* that they're excited by the news of the pending breakthrough. That gives the audience a good feeling about itself. Note also how the daily job of reading the reports places the speaker in the center of the foundation's activities, thus establishing the necessary credentials to speak on the subject—and also giving the audience an "insider's" viewpoint, which almost everyone is delighted to have.

Once again, you must give the "I know my subject" signal as early in the talk as possible. As you can see, it lends itself to a neat interweaving with the other signals. That's always the goal; it's the total effect that counts.

SIGNAL NUMBER FIVE: "HERE IS MY MOST IMPORTANT POINT"

When I'm not traveling, I always watch the same local newscast while having breakfast. I suppose a lot of people who watch that show have the same problem I do: always missing the weather forecast. Why? Because it's given in 10 seconds, and it always follows a commercial. When the forecast comes on, I'm mentally tuned out. By the time I'm tuned back in again, the forecast is over!

That's a very common occurrence. Because of the ease with which we can slip into daydreaming, we tend to tune out when something isn't holding our rapt attention. And very few speakers can hold an audience's rapt attention at *all* times. Frankly, I don't think anyone can. There are just too many times when a particular word or phrase will send people off into a little world of their own. Say "mother," for example, and half the people in your audience will suddenly say to themselves, "Gee, I haven't called my mother in a while—better do it tonight."

The onus is on you, therefore, to make your audience tune in when you get to the most important point of your talk. In fact, if you *don't* do this, many people will get mad at you for having shortchanged them. After all, why were they sitting there in the first place?

Here are three different examples of the signal:

> *If you don't take anything else away from my talk today, I hope you'll remember this one point* [signal]. *It is, in fact, the key thought* [reinforcing signal] *that I came here to deliver:*
>
> *There's an important message* [signal] *in all of this that I hope you'll bear in mind in the future. Here it is* [reinforcing signal]:
>
> What I'm building up to, of course, is that only one conclusion [signal] *can be reached from the evidence—and perhaps you've reached the same conclusion* [reinforcing signal] *yourself. . .*

Note that the signal is always delivered in *two* parts, and with good reason: it takes a second or two for people to snap out of a reverie, if that's where they've been. You want to give them the extra time to catch up. Don't worry about sounding redundant; you won't. You're simply extending a common courtesy to the audience by signalling that this is the part they should hear—even if they haven't listened to anything else.

Having said this, the question now becomes, "What *is* your central point?" Perhaps you think that your talk will have *many* points, and that it's impossible to single out any one of them as more important.

Nope, think again. All messages, written or verbal, have one single point. In the Declaration of Independence, the message to King George III was: "We're free!" The Magna Carta said: "We have rights!" And the Constitution says: "Here are the rules." All three are complex documents, but all three have a *single* focal point.

In a campaign speech, the successful politician always knows the single message to deliver, no matter what the audience. It can be summed up in four words: "I'll work for you." Sure, the farmers are told all the details of how, where, and under what circumstances. So are the unions, and the business executives. But the single focus of these details is always the same. "I'll work for *you* (if you'll elect me)!"

Has the Women's Club asked you to give a short talk on gardening? If so, you'll probably tell them that gardening is fun, can save money, is healthful, relaxing, and gratifying. Central message: Take up gardening! Or maybe you've been asked to talk about municipal bonds. They're tax-free, usually safe investments, and have a ready market in case you want to sell. Message: if you have extra money available, consider municipal bonds as an investment. And so forth . . .

But sometimes the central theme is *not* your most important point. Let's drop in on the Women's Club meeting and see what the speaker *really* has to say about municipal bonds:

> . . .*so municipal bonds can be an excellent investment. But that's not always the case . . .and that's where a person like myself can be helpful. A professional investment counselor will look at your entire situation—your income, cash needs, tax bracket, and lots more—before giving you investment advice. So, I hope you'll leave here this evening with this one message; this one piece of advice from your friend, Jane Adams. Before you invest anywhere, get the help of a professional.*

Now you can see the most important point in this talk: it's, "If you're thinking about investing, give Jane Adams a call." The Women's Club invited her because they wanted to hear about municipal bonds, but she *accepted* because she wanted to sell Jane Adams.

Never lose sight of your most important point. If it's not the actual theme of your talk, make sure everyone knows what it *really* is. And if the most important point is *you*, do what Jane Adams did: highlight the service you (or people like you) can provide to your listeners.

Occasionally, a talk will require something I call "Multiple-Action Points." I generally don't like acronyms, but MAP's is especially handy. MAP's are the actions you want your audience to take in order to reach your goal. For example, a committee trying to save a wildlife refuge might want to persuade people to donate money to the cause *and* write to their representatives in Congress. In this instance, the most important point is to save the land, because if you don't sell that idea, you're not going to get *any* action. Here's how to construct the signal—and the MAP's:

> . . . *so I hope you'll all agree with me that it will have been worth coming here tonight* [signal], *braving this cold, winter evening* [reinforcing signal], *if we make a start toward saving the preserve. And we can do that in two ways* [organizing signal]: *by building an adequate war chest, and by alerting our people in Washington to what's going on.*

Note that the MAP's follow right on the heels of the important-point statement. And that's where they belong. In this way, you maintain the audience's full attention while telling them what you'd like them to do. The details of how *much* of a war chest you need, and what the letters to Washington might say, should follow next. (By the way, never insult your audience by suggesting they don't know the names of their representatives in Washington—or the state capital. It's true, many people don't; but I'll show you how to avoid this pitfall in the section on hand-out materials.)

Obviously, the most-important-point signal is the key item in your talk. Without it, all the other signals (and even a rip-roaring finish, which we'll get to next) are wasted effort. You're there for a *reason*—don't keep it to yourself.

SIGNAL NUMBER SIX: "I AM *FINISHED*"

From birth, we are taught that life has a definite, orderly rhythm; that everything has a beginning, a middle, and a conclusion. When the rhythm is broken, we can become very agitated indeed. Here's one of my favorite anecdotes:

Everyone is familiar with the seven-note musical ending that goes roughly like this: "DUM Dee-Dee-Dum-Dum DUM! DUM!" For ages, musicians have been using it to conclude a song or number that doesn't come to its own, logical conclusion—a sort of tacked-on, anything-to-get-outta-here sign-off.

Years ago, a bandleader friend of mine invited me to hear his band play a Friday evening dance at a nearby hotel. I arrived in the middle of a "set" to find the dance floor crowded and my friend very distraught—unusual, I thought, since the patrons looked happy.

"Everyone's talking and joking," my friend grumbled, "and no one's paying attention to what *we're* doing!" He turned to whisper something to his musicians, then turned back to me with a mischievous smile. "Watch," he grinned, "we'll fix 'em . . ." With that the bank launched into a short medley of popular show tunes, and, just at the conclusion, he turned to conduct a dramatic rendition of the aforementioned seven-note ending. Only it wasn't seven notes, it was *six*. The final DUM simply never came: the musicians put down their instruments and, to the astonishment of those in the suddenly dead-silent ballroom, left the stand for a break. My friend was all smiles. *"Now* they'll pay attention!" he said as he walked smartly away.

All of us go through life waiting for that final DUM. When it appears, right on schedule, we're reassured—the activity has come to its logical conclusion. And so it is with public speaking. Just as every stage performer must have a finale for the act, you *must* have a solid finish. The audience is waiting for it, wants it, and will show their appreciation when it arrives—provided it's right on schedule!

That schedule, of course, is up to you—but you must *signal* it to the audience so that they, too, know what the schedule is. The most common treatment of this is with "finally," a word frequently abused by speakers who are *nowhere* near their actual finale. I beg you, don't ever do that yourself. As I said before and will say again, audiences do *not* like to be fooled! "Finally" means, "Here it comes, folks—get ready to applaud!" Never use it in any other way.

Here are some other time-tested final signals:

> *I want to leave you with this one last thought . . .*

> *You've been a great audience, and before I take my exit bow, I'd like to show my appreciation by . . . [giving you my thought for the day; sharing a little "inside" story; etc.]*

(After a short pause from the main body of your

talk:) *Years ago, something happened to me that I'd like to share with you as a parting shot . . .*

Of course, there are lots more. The important point is that the signal must be upbeat and *positive*—never use a signal that denotes a restriction or negative feeling about yourself or your speech. In particular, avoid: "Well, I guess you're anxious to get on with other things." Even if they are, it will leave a bad taste in their mouths. Or, "I see I'm out of time, so I'll . . ." Even if you *are* out of time, the audience will feel cheated.

Also, notice that the signal is always *followed* by something else; a thought for the day, or a little story. A famous classical conductor of years past had the well-known habit of concluding his concerts with short, but exciting, orchestral works: thus, a heavy Beethoven symphony was always followed by a rousing march or a spirited overture to send the audience into the night air. He called these short pieces "lollipops," a term that needs no further explanation. Every audience deserves a lollipop!

A lollipop, however, is *not* a joke. For reasons I'll explain soon, it's very difficult to use humor properly these days. True stories taken from life, on the other hand, make great lollipops—as long as they are appropriate to the moment. They *involve* the audience and usually build nicely toward the conclusion—just the effect you want. The story of my bandleader friend is a good example.

On several occasions, I've been asked why my advice about closings runs contrary to the suggestion made by others that a concluding statement should always repeat the speech's main point. My answer is that if you haven't made your central point by now, you'll *never* get it across. Repetition means only that you haven't done your job properly. Give the audience something *different*—an extra bonus that they're not expecting. It will strengthen your overall message and prepare the audience for the *final* words you have to say.

And those words should always be words of thanks—regardless of the type of audience, or its size. Thank them for giving you their time and, if it's appropriate, thank the program sponsors for inviting you. Here's an example:

> *My thanks to Joe Green for inviting me to participate in the program today, and my special thanks to you. Not only have you been a great audience, but you've made my stay with you a delightful experience in every way. Thanks again, and have a terrific convention . . .*

Finally, a lollipop for you:

Show people are marvelous concluders. They know from long experience that the way you "get off" can color the entire impression the audience takes away from the theater. Learn from them. Your TV set is a constant seminar on the art of concluding. Watch the way the performers signal; the way they gesture; the way they always do something upbeat before taking that final bow. That's not "milking" the audience, it's giving them *exactly* what they want—a logical, exhilarating, totally positive conclusion.

Don't cheat your audience *or* yourself: They want to applaud, because it's part of the fun of being an audience. And you want to hear it because that's the reward for doing a good job. So give the signal, and

CONCLUDE CONCLUSIVELY!

A Speaker's Guide to Why and Where

Now that you have a much better grasp of the view from the audience, it's time to examine specific types of speaking situations—first by the general topic you'll be addressing, and then by the type of function where you'll be appearing.

As you're going to see the Six Signals are only a start toward effective communication with the audience. Depending on the situation, you'll require other, more specific signals to keep the audience completely involved in your talk.

Even if only one of these categories applies to your present situation, I urge you to read this section in its entirety. All public speaking chores overlap in many ways, and a principle explained under one heading may apply to others as well. And you never know where tomorrow may take you. Read it all.

Sharing Your Expertise

By far, the greatest number of public speaking opportunities fall to the individual who's acquired expertise in a specific field of endeavor. Whether it's your full-time pursuit or just your hobby, chances are someone wants to know more about it. But don't make the mistake of assuming that it's *this* particular audience: when an upcoming meeting slot remains unfilled, some program chairmen will grab for any available topic.

Far more serious are the potential problems that revolve around the audience's prejudices and preconceptions. Whether they relate to you personally, to your topic, or your general vocation, you must recognize them in advance and deal with them immediately.

Let's start with the case of a longtime member of a women's club who's been asked to speak on her favorite subject for the very first time:

> *I know many of you think of me as Grace Steel, grandmother—and that's fine; it's a role in life that I cherish. But for a few minutes today* [time signal], *I'd like you to think of me as Grace Steel, collector and lover of rare books. I've been deeply involved in this activity for most of my adult life* [expertise signal], *and, in fact, some of my best friends don't know that I spend virtually every Saturday at a book auction or fair somewhere in the country.*

Notice how the speaker has recognized her "identity crisis" and dealt with it in just a few short seconds. She has transformed the audience's mental image of her into that of an involved (and presumably knowledgeable) collector who jets off around the nation every week in pursuit of her avocation. Having broken down the audience's preconceptions, she now has a room full of potentially attentive listeners. Notice, too, that she has accomplished this without trampling on any of the members' feelings: her opening statement allows plenty of room for the person who *already* knows about this interest of hers—and conversely, doesn't make the other members feel that she has deprived them of an important piece of information all these years. After all, some of her best friends don't know.

Preconceptions about a *topic* frequently revolve around the fact that, at first glance, it seems dull and lifeless. Nothing turns an audience off faster than the expectation that they're in for a long, boring dissertation on a specialized subject. Once again, it's up to the speaker to anticipate and deal with this problem, *quickly.* Here's Grace Steel again:

> *I don't know if I can get all of you as interested as I am in the books themselves, but I would like to share with you the thrill of the chase—the raw excitement that flows into your body when you know you're hot on the trail of an original Beethoven manuscript or a long-lost edition of* Marlowe's Faustus *that even the British Museum doesn't have.*

Here, the speaker breathes life into her topic, giving it motion, animation, and a whiff of international intrigue that the audience can relate to. And once again, she does so without treading on their sensibilities: she recognizes that not everyone shares her passion for the books themselves—without putting down the audience for their lack of interest.

Let's hear the remarks of another speaker with the same

general problem, but in an entirely different field:

> *When Len first called me and asked if I'd come speak with you today on the subject of lighting in the modern office, I said to myself, "Gosh, how am I ever going to get a diverse group like this one interested in such a specialized topic?" And then it dawned on me that at one time or another, all of us face the problem of getting out of bed and motivating ourselves on a grey, overcast morning. And I thought you'd like to know why that is—and how lighting affects our personal performance in many different ways.*

Clever, don't you think? The speaker has taken a *very* narrow subject area and immediately related it to everyday life—and a very common challenge that nearly all of us face.

A third area of prejudice—and another one that all of us share, in one way or another—relates to a person's *vocation*. Many of these stereotypes are fed to us by movies and television: the absent-minded college professor or the sloppy, unkempt sports reporter:

> *I know many of you think that those of us who cover the sports beat are a bunch of pseudo-jocks who lounge up there in the press box guzzling beer and banging out metaphors on cruddy old Underwood portables. Ah, if life were only that simple! Have you ever tried, for example, to balance a typewriter on your lap and type out a half-decent story while the plane you're on is doing loop-the-loops through a hailstorm? It seems we get to do that about twice a month. Or how about trying to find something—anything—to ask a star athlete that other reporters haven't asked him or her a hundred times before. Or a thousand times before . . .*

In this case, the speaker is bucking a common image of a profession that most of us really know little about, except what we read in the papers. And the message is simple: there's something unappealing about virtually *every* job, sportswriting included.

No matter what *your* job or topic, the audience is bound to have some preconceived notion that you'll have to deal with—and quickly—if they're going to hear and absorb the real message you came to deliver. Discover what it is; then attack it head-on.

But whatever you do, please don't *create* a new prejudice to take its place. In America, the word "expert" is starting to take on pejorative connotations. We live in a highly sophisticated society, with information on virtually every subject increasingly available at the push of a button or the turn of a dial. In a few years, many of our homes and offices will have videotex capability—a new technology that can deliver millions of facts via our television sets, on demand. The "expert" at the other end will be a computer, primed with the knowledge of thousands of specialists in each field from around the glove. That's a very tough act for any human being to follow.

The modern speaker must allow for the possibility that a goodly chunk of the audience may have already learned a large amount of information on the topic from other, perhaps inanimate, sources. Some out there may know *more* than you do (or at least think they do). Either way, you don't want to present yourself as infallible, because none of us are—and none of us are fond of people who think *they* are. In fact, that's one reason we usually stop listening. Being an expert and having expertise are *not* the same thing. Make your audience aware that you know the difference.

SELLING THE PRODUCT

When products are sold at meetings, the overwhelming majority of audiences are composed not of consumers, but of the middlemen who will be doing the selling—directly or indirectly—to the ultimate consumer. In other words, retailers, or the "sales reps" who call on retailers.

Here are two true stories. The names of the two companies involved aren't important, though anyone familiar with the inside stories will recognize them instantly.

These two companies faced similar challenges. Each had a new product it wanted to introduce to the marketplace: each product had an existing competitor already on the shelves, and each had an identifiable deficiency when compared with its existing competition.

Here's what the first company did: It sent a management team around the country to interview a large cross-section of retailers. The team returned with two vital facts: 1) the existing product was in very short supply, and 2) dealers' profit margins were so thin that hardly anyone was making money on the sale of the existing product, even when they *could* get supplies. Armed with this information, top management ordered production to proceed full-tilt so that the warehouses would be completely stocked before the new product's introduction. They devised a pricing schedule that guaranteed a profit on every retail sale. And they planned a series of modest sales meetings where the retailers were told exactly *what* had been decided and *how*. The company disclosed one last crucial fact to the retailers: it *knew* it had a problem with the new product and was working on an improved model that would eliminate the deficiency.

The introduction was a huge success.

Here's what the second company did: It hired a high-powered media company to devise a razzle-dazzle series of new-product introduction parties around the country. The plan for each party consisted of an hour-long open bar with hot *hors d'oeuvres,* showing of several expensive TV commercials designed to introduce the product to the public, and a number of speeches by the company's top brass, who decided to concentrate on the long-term sales projections for the new product and avoid even the slightest hint that a deficiency existed.

The parties themselves were a great success. But the retailers' initial orders were less than half of what the company had expected.

Of course, other factors were also present in the marketplace. But there's no doubt that the *approach* to the audience played a major role in the initial product introductions. In the first instance, the audience's collective ego was stroked and boosted by a company that paid attention to the retailers' complaints. In the second instance, the grass-roots problems were simply ignored.

The collective ego of a sales audience *always* tells it that the people in the seats understand the complexities of the marketplace far better than the people at the podium. While this may not always be true (some executives have made an art form out of keeping their ears to the ground), it's nevertheless a potent force within the meeting room. Contrast these two different approaches to an audience:

> *My friends, not only is this the finest model we've ever produced, but I absolutely guarantee that your customers are gonna love it! By gosh, I can't tell you*

how excited we are at headquarters by this year's entry . . .

You told us last year's model had a problem—and we listened. Thanks to you, this year's entry is the finest thing in the marketplace. But we still want your input! We may be the best right now, but the competition's hot on our trail—and we're not about to get complacent. Call me. And if the problem's not in my department, I'll get whoever's department it is, and we'll both listen . . .

Judging strictly from the approach, I don't think there's any doubt which product will get the best reception. When the speaker and the audience become *partners,* there's almost no limit to the good things that can happen.

There's one more thing you should remember about sales meetings. Actually, it applies to all types of meetings, whether the item being pitched is a product or a service (which we'll discuss next).

Successful salesmen justifiably see their job as *selling.* That's what pays the rent, regardless of whether the staff is on straight salary or a commission basis. As far as they're concerned, the key to success is *more* sales—not listening to you. They don't mind meeting with you to learn about a new product, service, or technique, but when they're hearing just the same old pitch one more time, they can get m-i-g-h-t-y angry. Sometimes that anger is very well hidden, but trust me, it's still there.

So be warned: Signal Number One is vital at sales meetings, especially those held during normal business hours. Give it immediately, and stick to your promise. You'll have an attentive and appreciative audience—if you really have something to say.

SELLING A SERVICE

At first glance, you might think that using a meeting to sell a service would be harder than employing the same meeting to sell a product. After all, a product can be exhibited and demonstrated, and the service can't.

But actually, it's the other way around. In our visually-oriented society, products don't lend themselves to verbal descriptions—but services do. In fact, they're just about perfect for the meeting-room atmosphere. The *way* a service is presented, however, is crucial. Make a mistake, and your time is wasted.

Audiences don't want to be told what a service *will* do, they want to be told what it *can* do. Here are two examples:

> *Our life annuity will insure that your retirement years are trouble-free and available for the things you really want to do. And best of all, the cost is very modest compared to the benefits.*

> *I think you'll find it very worthwhile to explore our life annuity. It can provide excellent retirement benefits, and most people find the cost surprisingly modest when compared with the long-term results.*

Look pretty much the same? They're not. The first example is a *will* statement and doesn't take into account that audiences are composed of many different individuals. The second example is a *can* statement, in which the key word is "explore." It speaks directly to the *individual*, not to the group as a collective unit. Audiences don't buy life annuity policies, individuals do.

The world becomes more impersonal every day. In many

ways, we must accept that fact and go on living. But when a choice exists, every one of us will opt to be recognized as an individual human being with unique attitudes, tastes, and needs. We ought to inscribe that doctrine on the door of every meeting room in the land, so that every speaker could see it on the way in.

You *must* talk to the needs of the individual. You must recognize that the room is filled with many different viewpoints—and phrase your appeal in a way that leaves no doubt that you do. Majority rules the audience's attitude toward the speaker, but it does *not* sway the individual wallet. Please remember that, whether you're selling life insurance, real estate, travel, maintenance, security, information, or any other service.

It's often said that selling is most successful when the appeal is directed toward the emotions—particularly the perceived needs for status, acceptance, security, comfort, and shelter. That's sound advice, as long as you also take into account that many audiences are much smarter than some speakers give them credit for. Emotional appeals work only when they don't insult the audience's collective intelligence. Here's a good example, from a salesman for a home-security firm—one of the more "emotional" services on the current market:

> *If you'll give us the opportunity, we'd like to come to your house and make a survey of all the doors, windows, and other points of possible entry. While I can't promise that we can offer a vast improvement in your present situation, the visit is free, and we may find things that you yourself have overlooked.*

Note the clear-cut emotional threat in the words, "other points of possible entry." Yet the speaker does not insult the intelligence of a prudent homeowner who has safeguards already in place. Notice, too, that the appeal is entirely personal and individual: "*your* house" and "things that you *yourself* have overlooked."

Always bear in mind the limitations on information that arrives in verbal form. When selling a service, it's best to handle details in a general way, so that the audience is not burdened with too many items to remember. Here's the representative of a large real estate firm who's flown up for the evening to address the employees of a company that's relocating to his home state:

> *I know you're going to enjoy living in Brightspot; it's a planned, energy-efficient community that features many enjoyable leisure-time activities. We have a lovely lake, and a terrific outdoor concert facility that's open year-round. But rather than give you a long [time signal] list of our attractions, I'd like to invite you to see the town with one of our representatives. We'll take each one of you on a personal tour, so you can see all the available homes in your taste and price range, and also all of our public facilities . . .*

There's an offer that's hard to refuse. The speaker has given just enough information to whet the appetite—but not enough to cause any confusion about the basic sales pitch: "We'll help you purchase your new home."

Selling a service in a group setting is a marvelous way of doing business: it's very efficient when compared to individual sales calls; and after the meeting concludes, the speaker gets an opportunity to talk to individual prospective clients. But do make use of all the signals, Number Two and Number Four in particular. You must tell them you *know* who they are, and never forget that the burden's on you to establish your credentials.

TALKING TO THE TROOPS

Modern communications are a two-way street, and on the door of every company conference or meeting room they should hang this sign:

DON'T TALK UNLESS YOU'RE PREPARED TO *LISTEN!*

Employee groups' most frequent complaint is exactly that—that managers want to talk, but don't want to listen. Some people even suggest that's one reason why the Japanese, with their interlocking system of management/ employee dialogue, are beating the pants off us in a number of industries.

I don't believe the work ethic is dead in America; I know too many people who work very hard indeed at what they do. But I do think that many of us—managers and employees alike—are having one heck of a problem with our job-role identities. Too many wagons are tightly circled around the campfire; too many people feel personally threatened by what should be considered honest and valid criticism. In that kind of atmosphere, no one's going to communicate with anyone.

Here's what one manager did about it:

I want to take a few minutes this morning to talk about the way we communicate with each other. Last night, someone put an unsigned note on my desk saying that our quality-control would continue to stink, until I stopped beating the drum for increased output and started paying attention to the number of defect-returns we're getting from the retailers. And I want that person to know that I think he—or she—is right. Someday, I hope that person will walk into my office and say, "I wrote that note," because by that time, our quality-control is going to be second to none, and I'm going to want to shake that person's hand!

Now, here's what the manager *could* have said:

As you all are very well aware, our quality-control stinks up a tree! Now, that's just not gonna fly around here anymore, people. We're either gonna get that line into shape, or changes are gonna be made—and fast! I'm not gonna bust my chops to make excuses for this department anymore.

Two verbal messages, both about the same problem, but each with a different—and unmistakable—intent. Message number one is: "Thank you for reminding me that quality is also my responsibility." Message number two is "Anyone who thinks they're gonna blame this mess on me has another think coming!" Which one signals the employees in a positive manner and opens the door for further interchange and cooperation? Not even a close call, is it?

In one respect, human beings are not too far removed from animals: when one of us senses the presence of a threat, the rest of us get the message very quickly. "Something's wrong! Run for the trees! Protect yourself!" If that's the message you want to pass along to your subordinates, all you have to do is act threatened yourself—they'll take the hint. If, on the other hand, you want your message to read, "Something's wrong. Let's work at it. We can make it right," then you have to examine your signals. Is that what you're *actually* sending?

An old army saying states that both the privates and the generals put on their combat trousers one leg at a time. There's a philosophy there we would all do well to remember.

FUND-RAISING

When it comes to fund-raising, the most frequently overlooked rule is a point we've made before: audiences do not exist in a vacuum.

Each of us likes to think our favorite charity is the most worthwhile, but that's not the way the world works. Members of any one audience contribute to *many* different charities, and a lot of people who do fund-raising for these charities are also out there in the seats. The question is, are you saying what they want to hear?

If your appeal sticks to the facts and imparts to the audience a sense of participation, your chances are excellent. As an audience, we want to know *what* you're doing, *who* you're doing it for, *why* it needs to be done, and *how* we can help—but that's all. Nobody wants a long harangue about how high the deficit is this year! Every nonprofit organization is having its problems, and many of us have become very proficient at reading balance sheets stained with red ink—all too often, those of our own companies.

And we *particularly* don't want to hear about your cutbacks. This doesn't give us a positive reason to participate, it only reminds us of the frustration of our own financial inadequacies. So just tell us how the money will be used, not how many people will suffer because we aren't philanthropic millionaires and can't give more.

Finally, we want you to recognize that we're involved and

concerned—otherwise, we wouldn't be here listening to you. That makes sense, doesn't it? So why not acknowledge that we're all involved with *other* charities, too, and are splitting our limited resources into a number of worthwhile pots? And why not acknowledge that we hear a lot of other speakers, just like you, telling us how badly our money is needed? And that when we leave here, someone else is going to request our contributions. . .

I've been to any number of fund-raising affairs, and have seen too many turn counterproductive in their zeal to raise cash. One of the most offensive features of some gatherings is the parade of speakers who, one after the other, try to outdo each other at the podium. That's not charity talking, that's each speaker's individual ego saying, "Watch me—I'll raise more money than those other slobs!" It's a pity: I've watched good people—who *would* contribute and stay involved—walk out of the room, vowing never to return.

The rules that govern fund-raising audiences are no different from those applying to all *other* audiences. Heed them. Give us a match between what you want to say and what we want to hear. If you do, we'll dig as deep in our pockets as we can. If you don't—well, I'd rather not think about it.

Having outlined the *why,* let's go on to the *where.* The following categories are divided by type of function, and not type of facility, because in most cases the former determines the latter. Most food functions are held in hotel ballrooms. Everything else can be held practically anywhere, from an in-house corporate conference area (which could vary from a corner of the cafeteria up to a full-blown auditorium) to a school building or church basement. But knowing the facility isn't nearly as important as knowing the *function*—and the corresponding type of audience you can expect to be present.

BREAKFAST MEETINGS

Try this on for size: It's 7 A.M. on a workday morning, and you're in your pajamas at the kitchen table, staring at a soggy bowl of Snappo-Crispies through lead-weighted eyelids. Suddenly the kitchen door flies open, and in marches a black-tuxedoed *maitre d'*, a helper pushing a podium on wheels, and a group of executive types wearing Brooks Brothers suits and white carnations.

You try to mutter a feeble protest, but to no avail: the *maitre d'* whisks away your bowl of cereal, the helper sets up the podium, and 30 seconds later, the first of the executive types has launched into an elongated presentation on "The Power of Keynesian Theory on an Unregulated Marketplace."

Far-fetched? Actually, it's a pretty accurate description of how most audiences perceive breakfast meetings. If you're scheduled to make a presentation at such a function, you'd better know that *right now.*

Breakfast meetings are deadly—especially when scheduled for the morning after a big convention bash. If you find half the seats filled, consider yourself lucky. Consider yourself luckier if anyone is paying the slightest attention to anything besides the location of the nearest pot of coffee.

Even when the breakfast meeting is a free-standing event not connected to a convention, problems abound. Many business people simply refuse to attend such functions on workday mornings. Those who do—often because they are obligated in some way to the program sponsors—are almost totally preoccupied with whatever problems are waiting on their office desks. That becomes *your* problem, particularly if you're scheduled to make an important presentation. But worst of all, the breakfast audience views you as a threat before you even open your mouth. In their eyes, you're the long-winded S.O.B. who's gonna run on and on, heedless of the clock, forcing them either to depart before you're finished (calling attention to themselves in the process, which is even more unpleasant when the program sponsor is watching) or else stick it out till the bitter end.

Breakfast meetings are fine for awards and acknowledge-ments—small-chore presentations which, by their very nature, are fast, simple, and require little except perfunctory applause. Otherwise, avoid them like the plague!

MORNING MEETINGS

These are the sessions held between 9 A.M. and noon, or until the lunch break. At conventions, a morning meeting can consist of a session for the entire attendance or several sessions (called "breakouts") for smaller groups, divided by topics or membership categories. A session can last for a short period or for the entire morning—in which case a coffee break is usually inserted around 10:15 A.M.

Most experienced speakers and seminar leaders (myself included) greatly prefer morning sessions. For one thing, you're getting the audience fairly early in the day. They've been exposed to a minimum number of outside influences and therefore can give you excellent attention. Although individual energy levels vary, most people hit a peak around midmorning, and this too works in your favor. But best of all, morning audiences are there because they *want* to be there: either they have chosen your session over an alternate convention offering (or recreational activity), or they've come in from the outside—which means they consider your session more important than their normal duties. More than that, a speaker just could not ask.

However, some peculiarities about the morning should be taken into account. During the first session of the day, hotel meeting rooms are at their coldest temperature. This can create immediate audience discomfort that will detract from the attention level. When things are *really* chilly, a participant will often interrupt the proceedings to ask that the thermostat be adjusted—which can start a little debate among members of the audience as to how cold and uncomfortable it really is. If you're the day's first speaker, ask your hosts to inquire about audience comfort *before* the session gets officially under way.

The first session may also be late in getting started—from either a breakfast affair that has run late or a large number of late-arriving attendees. Either way, it creates several problems. People who have arrived on time can get very annoyed when they're kept waiting in their seats (and they're right), which creates an unfavorable atmosphere for the first speaker. And later speakers on the program may suddenly find that their time allotment isn't anything like what they were originally promised.

If you're scheduled for the morning, ask how much time you'll have, and then plan to use *less*. If you're the last of several speakers before the lunch break, make that a great deal less!

A few words about the coffee break are also in order—particularly if the audience knows the break time in advance. If you're scheduled to speak immediately before the break, you must pay careful attention to the clock—or have someone else do it for you; a subject we'll cover later on. Many people consider their mid-morning cup of coffee a sacrosanct ritual, and will become annoyed and impatient if you deprive them by running over into *their* scheduled break period.

I've saved the most important warning for last. Morning audiences can get *very* annoyed with disorganized speakers who waste time. Because the collective energy level is high, the audience feels it has the right to stimulating and exciting presentations—and displays a very low tolerance for anything else. Now that you have the Six Signals, *use* them! Your audience will thank you. And if you're the first speaker on the program, your fellow speakers will also thank you. Everyone loves a dynamite opening act!

LUNCHEONS

When a luncheon is in the hands of a first-class meeting planner *and* a top-drawer hotel banquet staff, the results can be exceedingly pleasant: a smoothly-run affair that begins and ends on schedule and provides a very welcome break in the day's activities. That should be the norm, but it isn't. The average luncheon begins late, ends even later, and has the full potential to become a royal pain for everyone involved. I know many business people who, short of *force majeure* (which is French for, "They'll have to twist *both* arms!"), just won't go to luncheons anymore. I can't blame them.

Hotels, you see, are in the business of selling lodging, food, and alcoholic beverages. Their biggest markups are usually on the booze; so given their druthers, hotel banquet managers want you to start every affair with a so-called "open" bar (the sponsor pays the tab for everything consumed). I don't blame the hotel people—that's their job. Problem is, it's virtually impossible to open an open bar at noon and close it down a scant twenty minutes later. Even if you start blinking the lights furiously at that point, there will still be people who haven't made it through the crowd for their *first* drink, and a lot more who want to get a refill before the thing closes.

So, the luncheon starts late.

The next item the hotel wants is to sell is food, and as much of it as they can. Whereas the menu in the hotel's regular restaurant will feature a variety of salads, sandwiches, and one-course hot entrees, the *banquet* menu always features four- or five-course extravaganzas, soup to nuts, as they say. Needless to add, it all takes time to serve. And so everything starts running even later.

And that's where you come in. A third of your audience wants to get up and take a stroll to help them digest a lunch that's twice the normal size. Another third wants to nap. And the rest just want to get the hell out of all the cigar smoke and back to their offices—or to whatever's next on the convention schedule. Lucky you!

On the other hand, if you like a good challenge, luncheons (unlike breakfasts!) are *not* impossible, just difficult. A tightly-edited, well-organized speech on the right topic will do the trick—provided you give it a snazzy delivery. That's going to take a lot of preparation and rehearsal, but it may be worth it. Nothing can raise your personal stock at a convention like a good luncheon speech. Good *dinner* speeches are usually forgotten overnight, but the same performance at a luncheon can make you the talk of the convention for the rest of the day.

Here's how to do it:

First, you need a dynamite topic. "The Coming Trends in Pension Fund Actuarial Planning" will *not* do the trick.

"How to Survive the 80s" just might. If you've been invited to speak at a luncheon, sit down with the sponsors and work out a topic that will grab the audience at the affair and grabs *you* right now. Then give it a lot of work and rehearsal (there's help in both areas coming up later). Plan to speak for twelve minutes, and not a second longer.

On the day of the speech, have a normal breakfast (nothing more, nothing less) and plan to take a nice brisk walk about an hour before show time. Then claim your seat at the headtable, tell the waiter to bring you just a salad (you don't want all that food weighing you down!), and wait for your introduction.

Afternoon Meetings

Afternoon meetings are a great place to have people *do* things. Action fights the natural lethargy that usually sets in, with or without a big lunch. Audience participation creates movement and energy that otherwise wouldn't exist.

The *worst* thing you can do in the afternoon is stand behind a lectern for an hour, reading a speech. Eventually, everyone in the room will get the nods.

If they want you as a speaker for a full-afternoon session, ask for the first spot on the program. If it's available, you'll get the audience right after they've had a little physical activity (the walk from the luncheon room, if nothing else) and before another speaker can put them in Never-Never Land. Remember, an audience that's daydreaming is very hard to jolt back to reality. Politely avoid any spot on the program that falls after 3 P.M. That's when most people begin to hit their energy trough for the day; and from there on out, the audience is preoccupied with getting free, having a drink, dinner, and enjoying their personal plans for the evening. Above all, avoid the last spot on the program—it's the pits!

Next, pay very close attention to the temperature. If it's on the warm side—as it's likely to be unless the room has been empty all morning—have someone lower the thermo-stat. The idea is to keep it just a notch below cozy at all times.

Above all, you must give your presentation rhythm and movement. It must march along in quick-step, taking your audience right along with it. This reduces the opportunity for daydreaming to a minimum and keeps the audience *involved*. Which means, of course, that *you* have to be on your toes, too—and that's the key to success in the afternoon. Monkey see, monkey do! Give your audience a superb role model. Before your turn behind the podium, take at least ten minutes outside in the fresh air. Breathe! Take a fast walk around the block to get the blood pumping a little faster. Above all, take your midday meal with plenty of moderation: a light salad or a big bowl of soup. Don't let your stomach weigh you down. You want to be light on the foot and fast on the wing.

That'll do the trick!

Cocktail Parties

Everyone in the business world has been to at least one cocktail party where they booze everyone up and then ask the boss to get up and say a few words.

A cocktail party speech that's anything more than a few perfunctory remarks is simply a waste of time. People won't stand and listen to anything at the close of the day, particularly not with drinks in their hands. Try as you may, they'll continue to chatter among themselves, kiss and shake hands with new arrivals, and just generally ignore you.

Save your energy. Do it somewhere else.

DINNER BANQUETS

This is the big enchilada—the main event, as they say. The good after-dinner speaker is one of the most sought-after commodities in the nation, because there just aren't enough talented people to go around.

You could become one of them—establish a reputation, and there's no end to the number of times your phone may ring. And it really isn't all that difficult. All you need is the *will* to make it and a clear understanding of the rules of the road. Here they are:

First and foremost, a banquet audience wants to be *entertained.* They've worked hard all day, and they've really earned it. That applies to *all* audiences, whether they're actually working people or not.

So you'll be expected to be entertaining. That *doesn't* mean you're going to get up and tell a couple of fast gags. That's entertain*ment,* and that's not what we're talking about. An entertain*ing* speech is one that gives the audience a whole *bunch* of lollipops: interesting facts they didn't know (especially about people or things in the headlines), or fascinating true stories or anecdotes that fit into your theme. It's work, and takes preparation, but it's well worth it.

A popular misconception is that banquet speeches should be long, drawn-out affairs. When a talk isn't entertaining, that's simply the way it *seems.* In actual fact, a good after-dinner speech just zips along and always leaves the audience wanting just a little bit more. (That, as you know, is one of the cardinal rules of show business.) Fifteen minutes—twenty at the very most—will do just fine.

Believe it or not, your introduction (covered later in the book) is one of the keys to your success. Work on it. Mark Russell says that one of the hardest tasks he faces on the banquet trail is an audience that's still waiting for its first laugh of the evening—and he encourages his introducers to try and break that ground for him. Follow his example, and write *yourself* a first-class introduction that really sparkles with anticipation—and try to have a first-rate associate rehearse it and give it. Even if you're not after laughs (and you usually aren't) you want to get lots of applause on the way to the podium.

All of this presupposes, of course, that you really *are* ready. Banquets pose obstacles that must be anticipated in advance. No matter what they set in front of you at the headtable, always eat with great moderation. A heavy meal takes time to digest, and, once again, you want to be as light on your feet as possible. Keep yourself lean, a little hungry—and ready to go!

But it's the booze, not the food, that should be your biggest concern. Don't touch a drop! I know, it looks *very* tempting, especially since you've got the jitters. But getting the jitters is part of the territory—and very few good speakers drink any alcohol before show time. Remember, alcohol is a *depressant*—exactly what you don't want.

The fact that most of your audience *has* been drinking should also concern you. Liquor can do strange things to people: some mellow out, others get very abusive. Bad drunks are *bad* drunks, whether in the banquet hall or anywhere else, and won't hesitate to get even for a real or imagined slight. Examine every word with a microscope. Could someone—especially someone who's been drinking—get upset or offended by this? If even the slightest doubt exists, get it o-u-t!

The hall itself is also an important consideration. Visit it well in advance. Familiarize yourself with every detail. Make that space yours, if only for one night. (We'll talk more about this later on.)

Most of all, bring along the very best *you*. If need be, take the day off. Ever feel refreshed, relaxed, and ready to give it all you've got after a full day on the job? Thought not! So play some golf or take a swim—whatever's going to put you in a top-drawer frame of mind. And good luck.

EVENING MEETINGS

Evening meetings are common to neighborhood associations, parent/teacher groups, and other community-based organizations where the membership isn't available until after the dinner hour. While these meetings almost always operate on a very informal basis, guest speakers are frequently invited to make formal presentations on a variety of topics.

After-dinner meetings present the speaker with serious challenges. Often, the physical setting is less than ideal: school classrooms, church basements, and community centers or clubs are favored sites, although almost anything with four walls and seating can be used. Voice amplification systems usually vary from fair to non-existent. A podium may not be available. And the speaker may be expected to address the group from either a standing or seated position. In the evening, the rule is expect anything.

Estimating attendance at any particular meeting is next to impossible. The same organization may provide a standing-room-only crowd for one speaker and a half-empty room for another. The size of any evening's audience is largely beyond the control of either the speaker or the sponsor: the weather, the season, the evening's TV schedule, and other organizations' conflicting events all play a part.

Obviously, the speaker and the topic do determine attendance to some degree, but even well-known politicians experience wide variations in turnout from one meeting to the next. In addition, the timing of the meeting announcement is critical—if it arrives too early, it is easily forgotten; too late, and the members have chosen other activities on that evening. Since almost all organizations depend on volunteers to do this work, the timing of the announcement (if one is even sent) is rarely anything close to perfection.

Make up your mind right now: no matter who *you* are or how "hot" your topic, you may have to face a lot of empty seats. Many speakers can't cope with that; they view empty seats as a comment on their personal worth, rather than looking at the situation objectively. That's a shame—it cheats both the audience and the speaker out of a meaningful evening. To add to the problem, some audience members (who want their decision to attend validated) can also be affected by the size of the turnout.

The problem, on either side, is not insoluble. Where folding chairs are used, the speaker can request that only half the normal number be set up in advance. That not only makes the crowd look larger, but also forces those who attend to sit closer together—providing greater enthusiasm through an increased sense of participation. As additional people arrive, more seats can be set out, which also gives the function a look of success.

A similar solution is available in classroom-type settings where the chairs are permanent, but movable. Here, the simple device of dividing the chairs into *two sections*—separated by a wide aisle—subtly influences most attendees to seek seats in the forward section. Even if the rear section remains empty, the audience looks larger than when people are spread out all over the room.

Because of the nature of evening meetings, people frequently arrive and depart while the session is in progress. Not only must you be prepared for these distractions, but it's vital that you understand that they're *not* a reflection on you or your performance. All evening audiences are under time pressures: children must be put to bed, babysitters taken home, public transportation schedules adhered to. Don't take it personally.

But the biggest problem in the evening is the audience's mood, coupled with that particular organization's general decorum. Some people have very short tempers when they're fatigued, and, because tolerance levels are low, seemingly minor issues can develop into major confrontations. This is particularly true at meetings where an "anything goes" attitude prevails: the audience ego says that members can argue with—even interrupt—the speaker whenever they choose. This can be disconcerting to say the least, especially to the uninformed visitor.

As with everything else in public speaking, the secret to success in the evening is being prepared. Learn everything you can about the organization itself and the way meetings are conducted. If possible, contact someone who has spoken to that same group in the past. Would that speaker do it again? If not, why? Forewarned is forearmed. You may decide to avoid what might be a nasty experience. Or you may decide that advance preparation will carry the day and that the effort's worth it. If so, make sure you follow through: get as much detail as you can about *exactly* what's on the membership's collective mind. Then beat them to the punch by including these details in your prepared remarks. It not only staves off questions from the floor but shows the audience you really care—which makes any group feel good about itself, and you.

When the
Telephone Rings

Fame and power do not guarantee that you'll be immune from life's little problems. Oliver Wendell Holmes discovered this once on a train ride when he couldn't find his ticket.

"That's all right, Mr. Supreme Court Justice," said the conductor, who had instantly recognized his famous passenger. "I'm sure the railroad can trust you to mail it in when you find it."

"My good man," replied an exasperated Holmes, "the question is *not*, 'Where is my ticket?' The question is, 'Where am I *going?*'"

When the phone rings and the caller asks if you'd like to give a speech to a group of people, that's the question you should ask yourself: Where am I going? Will it advance my career to take on this task? What risks are involved? How much work will it take to do a first-rate job? These and other questions should run through your mind before you say yes.

As you're now aware, knowing your audience is one of the tickets to success in public speaking: you must know who they are, what they want, and the types of problems they're facing. But that's only the start. In order to guarantee a trouble-free performance, you'll need the answers to other questions as well. Some may seem mundane, but all are extremely important.

WHO ARE THEY?

If you're already a member of the organization that wants your speech, no problem—you probably know all you need to know right now. In *all* other cases, you'll want a full rundown on the organization, and I suggest you get it *before* making any commitment.

In particular, you'll want to know the name of the group, how often they meet, their purpose (unless they're a well-known service organization like the Kiwanis, in which case you'd look foolish to ask), and the number of members.

An excellent source of information is friends who happen to be members. Ask around; it's possible you were recommended by a friend in the first place. Once you find a contact, get everything you can by way of "inside" information: who the members are, their age range, what they have in common, and so on.* Also ask for a realistic meeting

---

*Many clubs have a policy of inviting the guest speaker to lead a recitation of the Pledge of Allegiance—or the singing of the National Anthem or "God Bless America" before the meal, frequently without advance warning. Though it's not done as frequently, they may want you to give the invocation. Ask.

attendance figure—program chairmen are notoriously optimistic on this score, but a friend will give this to you pretty straight.

If it's a company meeting for which you're being sought, find out the *exact* nature of the company's business. You want to know their product line, whether they're regional, national, or international, and the names of any other interlocked companies within the corporate group. (You don't want to tell the audience you hate Dipsy-Cola, only to find out it's manufactured by a sister company!)

Get a complete rundown on the specific department or group you're being asked to address, and the names of all officers or managers who might be present in the room. Also obtain the name of the person in charge of the meeting (if it's not the same person doing the inviting—and sometimes it isn't).

If you're being asked to address a convention, you'll want complete information on the industry and/or trade association involved and a complete rundown on the membership categories. In particular, what type of function do they have in mind for you? Is it designed for all members, or for one particular class of membership? Many trade associations have a category known as "allied members," usually composed of firms or individuals from industries or fields *associated* with the industry in question (for example, the people who supply the main industry with parts).

Obviously you'll want the names of all the officers of the convention organization. Since it's possible they'll be installing new officers during the convention, get a complete list of these people as well (which will probably duplicate many names, if not titles, from the old list).

Finally, ask them to send you a complete convention kit.

If this is not yet available, ask for draft materials—particularly those related to the convention theme or motto. In short, ask for everything that'll help you zero in on the delegates, the industry, and the prevailing mood.

YOUR TOPIC

Whether it's your choice, or theirs, you'll want to discuss your topic *in detail* with the person who invites you. Be warned: misunderstandings are common in this area, so leave nothing to chance.

In particular, you'll want to know *why* they want you—or that particular topic. If it's a local organization or company, did some recent event trigger their request? (Fire prevention experts always get the most calls immediately after a fatal fire in the community.) If it's a convention, find out everything you can about the type of year the industry or group has just had—its profitability, problems, and pending actions—and once again, ask questions about how your talk fits into the general convention theme.

Of equal importance is how much the group *already knows* in your field and topic area. Have any speakers from your field appeared at recent meetings? If so, what did they talk about?

Finally, if your topic is going to require a greater in-depth understanding of the organization and its challenges, don't hesitate to ask for help. See if someone on the inside is available to give you a personal briefing: it can only pay dividends, and the group will respect you all the more for your professional approach.

THE PROGRAM

Obviously you'll want to know the exact type of function involved. But that's only the starting point. Get full particulars on the agenda and overall program length (including any time restrictions, such as another meeting or function following this event).

If they're planning to transact any business, find out whether it's simple committee reports or something that might require extended discussion. Many a speaker has waited and waited, only to find that most of the time allotted to the speech has slipped away in the debate over a motion or some other item of business.

If other speakers are scheduled to appear on the same program, insist on knowing who they are* and their topics. It's not unusual for an over-zealous program chairman to schedule two people from the same field—sometimes bitter rivals—for the same program. You'll also want to know the speaking order— if it's already set; otherwise, negotiate the best position for that type of program.

Finally, how much time is being allocated to each talk? If you think they're overscheduling for the amount of time available, be honest and tell them so. Perhaps they haven't called the other speakers yet, and can delete one in the interest of a better presentation on your part. If they're locked in, however, don't hesitate to say no. You're much better off

---

*I once had the honor of following Hubert H. Humphrey, one of the great orators of our time, to the podium of a national convention—something I didn't know I was scheduled to do till I got there. It's probably for the best that someone didn't tell me in advance: I'd probably have chickened out and missed an opportunity to talk to a great audience—which is what the "Happy Warrior" left behind for me. What an opening act!

declining (and they'll respect that) than accepting an inadequate amount of time.

Always bear in mind your practical limits. A twenty-minute speech from prepared text is a *major* speech (about 2,000 words) and requires much more advance preparation than a ten-minute talk. If you don't have that kind of preparation time available, settle for something less ambitious.

ARE YOU REALLY FREE?

Check your calendar for any possible conflicts on that day, and for several days before. Are there any out-of-town commitments that might delay your return to the city? In winter, bad weather can cause many flight cancellations. At the very least, you want to be back in town a full day before the event.

If the speaking date *itself* is out of town, don't accept before you've checked the travel schedules and assured yourself that seats are available in both directions. Many a would-be convention speaker has suddenly found that all the airlines have long since been booked by convention delegates. Once again, you'll want to plan on arriving *at least* a full day before you're scheduled to appear. But if you're crossing several time zones (to Europe, say, or the Orient), you'd be very wise to make it *two* days in advance, to allow for changes in your sleep and working hours. The speech isn't worth giving if you're going to look half-dead when they call your name.

DETAILS, DETAILS...

These are the last items you'll need to nail down. But make no mistake, they're all important:

Chances are, the function's being held in a hotel. Insist on knowing which *room* in that hotel. If a final selection hasn't been made, tell them to get back to you. If you're being asked to appear at a luncheon or dinner banquet, get the name of the person on the hotel banquet staff who's handling the booking. You'll see why in a few seconds.

If the event is not being held in a hotel, and you're not *positive* of the facility's location, get complete directions and, if possible, make a dry run a day or two in advance. The number of speakers who have gotten lost on the way to private meeting facilities is up there in the mega-millions.

Since you want to arrive *early* on the day of your talk, find out if someone will be there to let you in. At private facilities, the doors are sometimes kept locked until ten minutes before the event starts. That's not enough time. You'll need about twenty minutes inside, so make special arrangements.

Ask the sponsors to send you a draft copy of the meeting announcement *before* it's sent to the printer. Is your name spelled correctly? (What's the point of preparing a dynamite talk on mutual funds if no one can find you in the phone directory after the meeting?) Is your title accurate? The topic what you agreed to? Leave nothing to chance—errors in one or more of these areas occur all the time.

Most of all, you'll want to *inspect* the facility, especially if you've been asked to make a major speech. Call the hotel and make an appointment with the person at the banquet office. Say you're the guest speaker, and they'll be happy to cooperate. If the room's in use when you arrive, just tip-toe in and stand at the back.

I can't emphasize how important this is. In fact, it's one of the real secrets to success. Spend twenty minutes in the space, and you won't be a stranger anymore. It's *your* room. Now the *audience* will be the strangers. Just good old practical psychology, and it works!

Putting Your Act Together

At this point, you're armed with a great deal of information—a combination of what you've gleaned from this book, and what you've learned from the program sponsor. In fact, you're probably *better* prepared than many people who consider themselves "experienced" speakers. Experience is a great teacher, but if you're always asking the wrong questions (or none at all), you'll keep getting the wrong answers.

Now it's time to begin putting your act together. Don't fall into the trap of worrying about the actual words you'll be using. At this stage of the game, that's far less important than you think.

Every finished product is a sum of its parts and raw materials. If any one of these items is missing, final assembly cannot be completed. And a car with a missing window is just as unsalable as one with a missing motor. It's time to assemble your raw materials.

What facts will you need to put your point across? What specifics will your *audience* want to hear? What stories or other devices will help you turn your presentation into a lively, involving experience for the listener? You must answer these questions before you ever get near a first draft of your talk.

Here are the items you'll have to assemble:

YOUR FACTUAL FOUNDATION

Facts are the raw materials of communication. Without them, everything reduces to simple opinion. And no matter who *you* are—or who your *audience* is—mere opinion will not carry the day.

The best place to start looking for supporting materials is in your home or office, where, chances are, any number of books, magazine articles, trade publications, and other documents are available at your fingertips. Take a good look around; everything you need may be just a few feet away.

If not, the next best source is the public library, and best of all, it's probably as nearby as your telephone. In most metropolitan areas, libraries offer a computer-based, phone-in information service that can provide facts on thousands of subjects in a matter of minutes.

In addition, most libraries have a periodicals department offering a wide variety of magazines (with articles indexed by subject, which is really nifty), newspaper files on microfilm (again indexed by subject), and, of course, a completely cross-indexed card catalogue of books on thousands of subjects.

If your topic is business or trade-related, a so-called "mercantile library" of trade publications may be available in your area. A university, institutional, or privately-funded library may also have exactly what you need. When I became interested in a little-known black musician popular just after the turn of the century, a private library in my area turned up an actual program book from one of his 1912 concerts.

Once your facts are assembled, their method of *presentation* becomes crucial. People have a great interest in *people*, not things. The black musician's name was James Reese Europe, and he probably invented the style of popular music we call the fox-trot. I think that's certainly more interesting than the name of the library where I found his concert booklet. Try to relate *your* facts to actual individuals, living or dead. Always tell what the person did in terms that describe *action*. He *invented* that musical style. She *discovered* that chemical element. That's the stuff that'll involve your audience.

Statistics, by comparison, are extremely dull, and next-to-impossible for audiences to remember. Does anyone *really* want to know the exact number of people who attended last year's Indianapolis 500? They may not even care that the crowd was the largest in history. But tell them that the stands were filled to overflowing with screaming racecar enthusiasts, and the audience is *transported* to the actual event. See if you can make your statistics come alive in a similar manner.

One type of audience can cause a serious problem with the presentation of factual material. When the speaker knows that the boss will be there, it frequently leads to the preparation of what I call a "one-person speech," consisting not of facts the audience wants to hear, but of facts (or opinions) that the speaker *thinks* the boss wants to hear. For example, a sales manager presenting a new product to an audience of appliance dealers may tell them things they really *don't* want to know—only because the divisional vice-president is standing at the back of the room. That's very foolish. The ultimate test is whether the sales manager can *motivate* the listeners to order appliances, not how many fancy adjectives can be crammed into a ten-minute talk.

A good fact is the best servant a speaker ever had. To make *your* facts come alive, give them motion and animation. Present your audience with interesting, action-oriented material that they can really sink their teeth into.

THE BIG QUESTION ON QUESTION & ANSWER SESSIONS

If, following your talk, there may be a question-and-answer session—at your initiative, or at the program sponsor's request—now's the time to think about it, while you're still assembling your facts.

Personally, I'm totally against these sessions. They're anticlimactic, very difficult to get moving (silence reinforces silence, remember?), and likely to elicit questions of *very* limited interest—or ones purposely loaded to get you into an argument or display the questioner's great wisdom. That's a losing proposition on all counts.

I suggest you tell your program sponsor (just before you're introduced, so it won't be forgotten) that you'll be happy to be available for *private* questions after the session is *over,* but in the interest of time, you don't want to hold a formal Q & A session from the podium. I always do this, and it works.

On the other hand, if you feel you need such a session despite its limitations and drawbacks, then you'll have to prepare for it *now*. Carefully examine every fact and piece of supporting evidence in your talk to see where possible problems lie (something you should do in any event). Are you saying that people who drink shouldn't be permitted to drive—or that a driver who has had *too much* should be kept off the road? There's a difference. Are you saying that the statistics prove that all of those accidents were *caused* by drunk drivers, or that drunks were *involved* in those accidents? Be prepared, and get your facts straight. The audience's collective ego does not require *anyone* to give you the benefit of the doubt.

Unfortunately, no matter how well you prepare, there's always a risk that you will be caught with a misstatement. Errors *do* occur in reference materials. If this happens to you, don't try to bluster your way out of the situation. Your best course of action is apology. Admit your mistake (even if it really *isn't* yours), and move on. The important thing is to salvage the fruits of your hard work—namely, the speech itself.

THE WELL-CHOSEN METAPHOR

In contemporary writing, metaphors are frequently used to "punch up" facts and descriptions and make them more colorful. That would seem to make a metaphor the speechmaker's ideal device—but rules for the spoken word are different, as I have pointed out several times.

Think of a speech as a sleek, new jet aircraft. You, the pilot (speechmaker), aim your plane straight down the runway, headed for high-speed takeoff—when suddenly the aircraft veers onto one of the taxiways leading to the terminal. That's the effect a metaphor can create, and I've used a metaphor to describe it. If it started you thinking—even for an instant—about your last airplane trip, then that's the taxiway; and it leads to a dead end. Keep your subject pointed straight down the runway toward liftoff *at all times.*

Always remember that your audience will daydream at the slightest invitation. Describing the texture of a new fabric as "smooth as a baby's bottom" invites your listeners to daydream about family life—which is a lot more fun than thinking about textiles. If you need a metaphor, always use one close to home. "Smooth as *silk*" keeps the audience on the fabric runway.

THE WELL-TOLD STORY

Where a metaphor can lead to a dead end, a well-told story can give the listener an enjoyable *detour.* Because stories conform to the life-rhythm cycle of beginning, middle, and conclusion, they can easily lead back to your main highway. Select your story with care, and the conclusion will end the detour at the exact spot you want.

If facts are the raw material of communication, stories are the optional extras. A good story involves the audience and, again, gives your speech motion and animation. And the story needn't be a long one: to illustrate my point about libraries, it took only one sentence to tell you of my quest for information on Jim Europe.

Search your personal experiences—and those of your friends—for interesting and involving stories related to *your* topic. If you come up blank, ask a history buff to think of a possible story related to your theme. Perhaps you'll remember an anecdote or incident in a book or magazine article you've read. (You'll find a list of additional sources at the back of this book.) Somewhere out there may be the perfect story for your audience.

Remember, every audience deserves a lollipop.

THAT'S NOT FUNNY

Over the two decades since the death of Lenny Bruce in 1966, the nature of comedy in America has changed drastically. A hostile popular press labeled Lenny "sick" for his many (often brilliant) flights of on-stage fantasy, and he was constantly hounded by self-righteous police and judges for his occasional use of certain words. Nevertheless, he opened many doors, through which have come the likes of George Carlin and Richard Pryor to challenge us with even wilder (and equally brilliant) flights of fantasy and language. Perhaps Lenny himself would be shocked. "They *do* that, man? Every night?" Yes, they do—and to packed houses, and the frequent delight of critics.

But other things have changed, too. The occasional two-line ethnic joke notwithstanding, it's no longer acceptable to point humor at racial or religious minorities. Common references once deemed OK are now considered patently offensive— particularly by women, but also by many men. And nowhere is this more true than in the banquet hall. For Carlin, Pryor, and company are not our tastemakers. Our tastemakers are Mary Tyler Moore and Johnny Carson.

Earlier, we talked about Johnny Carson's influence on would-be speakers. Now it's time to examine his even more pervasive influence on audiences. For he is such a frequent visitor to our homes that we often fail to see the true nature of his comedy.

The butts of Johnny Carson's humor are threefold: the establishment, the regulars on his show, and himself. It has been said, and bears repeating, that if you want to know what's on the country's collective mind, watch Johnny. Because of his national stature, he can make social and polit-ical comments through comedy that might be considered highly inappropriate from the rest of us—save a Mark Russell, and one or two others. Thus he can use the behav-ior of the First Lady for comic material. Were you or I to do the same thing, in the same words, it would be considered in bad taste by many in a banquet audience. Here, Carson sets the standard by being the exception.

Part of the key, of course, is that the member of the estab-lishment who is the most frequent butt of Johnny Carson's humor is Carson himself. Hence, a monologue exchange that goes something like this:

> Carson: "I was at the supermarket today and . . ."
> McMahon: *"You* were at the *supermarket?"*
> *(Laughter)*
> Carson: *(with a twinkle in his eye)* "I went there just to get this joke . . . *(more laughter)* . . . but in a few seconds, I may be *sorry* I did!" *(still more laughter)*

In the world of Johnny Carson, the audience is *always* right, especially when a gag fails to click. In the world of Johnny Carson, the fact that superstars do not do their own food marketing is used to acknowledge that life, fortunately, provides many opportunities to laugh at ourselves.

And that *does* set our standards. After all, if one of the

most popular personalities of our time can laugh at himself, shouldn't the rest of us be able to do likewise?

Which brings me to something I call the "Harry Factor." "Mr. President! Mr. President!" shouts Harry from the floor of the men's club meeting, "I have an *important* piece of business!" Thirty seconds later, a slightly tipsy Harry is at the microphone and launching into "the one about . . ." in *very* explicit language. There are enough Harrys around to cause quite a problem for the inexperienced speaker waiting for his turn at the dais. While a Harry holds forth, the speaker thinks to himself, "Well, perhaps a little off-color humor is in order here . . ." It's not. Harry gets away with it because he's an insider. You're a stranger. The audience's collective ego says that the members do *not* laugh at dirty jokes told by strangers. And *that's* the Harry Factor. Don't ever let it fool you.

If you're looking for a laugh, take your lead from Johnny Carson: the best way to get it is at your own expense—as our business executive did earlier in this book.

As I've suggested several times, telling jokes of any kind is a dangerous business for the speaker. Legions of professional comics will attest that it's harder than ever to get a genuine laugh out of the audience. The reasons are many and, for our purposes, largely unimportant. But remember, an audience assumes that the speaker is putting his or her best foot forward at all times. A failed laugh at the beginning of your talk makes the audience wonder whether there's more substandard fare to come. It's a pity to ruin a good speech just because the joke isn't funny.

THE CALL TO ACTION— AND HANDOUTS

Whether your speech is going to call for multiple-action points, or ask the audience to take just a single step, you must carefully prepare the groundwork. Before the speech is drafted is the time to do it. Precisely how *much* money do you need? *Where* is each contribution to be sent? Is the address *correct?* How are the checks to be made out—in whose *name?* Do you have all the information you need? If not, who does?

One frequently-requested action is a letter to a public official. Here, your speech can imply the *tone* of the letter. But you must leave the actual words with each individual, or you'll insult your audience by suggesting that they don't know what to say or how to say it. On the other hand, preparing a sample draft letter to be handed out to people who *request* it can pay handsome dividends.

Some people haven't the foggiest notion how to contact public officials. But giving this information in the speech itself also suggests that the audience is stupid. And unless you're in a classroom, few people will have the means to take notes. Once again, you can accomplish this by way of a prepared handout.

Here's how to handle both items:

I know most of you will want to phrase your letter —if you choose to write one—in your own style. But should anyone need an idea or two to add to their own thoughts, we have a copy of an especially good letter drafted by one of your fellow members. It will be available right after the meeting concludes. Also, if you don't have the address of Congressman Jeffries handy, we have a printed form containing this information, as well as his phone number here and in Washington. Just check at the door on your way out . . . .

Not only will this approach offend no one, but your call to action has a far greater chance of success. Give people something to carry home, and your speech is strengthened by the power of the printed word.

A last word about handouts: the wise speaker *never* creates his or her own competition by handing out material that can be read *during* the talk. Curiosity is a very strong motive: people *will* read a handout at the first opportunity. Invite them to concentrate on you, not a piece of paper.

THE TEXT HANDOUT

There's one additional type of handout you should know about. It's your speech itself.

Outside the top echelons of the corporate community, not many people use text handouts, yet they offer many benefits. They can expand your audience far beyond the hall's limits. They provide the press with the complete (and *accurate*) text of your remarks (which is why corporate officers use them). And, for the right audience, they can make a nifty lollipop.

Here's a Nobel-laureate chemist talking to an audience of colleagues:

Ladies and gentlemen, you've been a superb audience; and to show my appreciation, I'd like to

offer each of you a little bonus. I don't know about
you, but when I return from these conferences, I'm
always astonished how few of my notes I can actu-
ally read. I guess it's because we're so afraid we'll
miss the next point, that we don't take proper time
on the notes for the last one. Well, this time you need
not fear: my associate is standing at the exit with a
complete transcript of my remarks—for those who
want it . . .

This principle can be adapted to many other situations.
It does cost money, but with the right group, it can be well
worth it (in public relations, if nothing else). But do be careful not to offend your audience's sensibilities. If your entire
talk made only one real point—and a simply understood one
at that—don't rub the audience the wrong way by suggesting they need a printed transcript to remember what you
said.

Most people think of the press as simply the daily news-
papers. But many fields are covered by an active trade press
as well. Trade publications are always in the market for good
speeches, and you may be missing a golden opportunity to
expand your audience to many times the number of people
in the room. Nothing fancy or costly is required: a photocopy
of your typed remarks will do nicely. For most functions,
about four or five sets will cover all the trade-press people
present.

But do allow for those who *aren't* there. Trade-press
reporters may be hard-pressed to decide which of a number
of concurrent convention sessions to cover. Should they decide not to attend yours, you can track them down and offer
an on-the-spot copy of your remarks.

In a few pages, we're going to begin actually drafting your

speech, a process that's accomplished in several logical steps. One stage is the simple procedure of converting your message from written to spoken grammar. The draft of your speech made just before this conversion is the one to use for printing/copying purposes.

There's one small danger, however, which I'd like to mention as this section's last item. If you'd like to hand out a reprint of your speech, do take care that this decision doesn't color your choice of words for the *listening* audience. Your first priority is to reach those people sitting in the room, and, once again, the printed word and the spoken word *are* different. The speech you want to draft is the speech you want to deliver, not the one you want to see printed in the trade press. That's simply a more readable version (though the exclusion of the informalities) of your *spoken* text.

Five minutes after the exit doors fly open, your audience will be headed toward a multitude of other activities. Let them spread the word that you gave a great account of yourself. Then others will *want* to read your remarks when they're reprinted.

And that's two audiences for the price of one!

Drafting Your Speech

Fear of the unknown affects virtually everything we do—at work, at play, and in our relationships with other people. It even influences our selection of places to eat. How much easier it is to choose a restaurant where you *know* the service and food will be OK, and the prices within reason.

When we tackle something new, that fear is almost always present in one degree or another. It's your first, and most formidable, speech-drafting hurdle. But I'll show you how to leap over it in less than a minute's time.

You have a job. You're a hard worker, put in long hours, and turn out superior results. Trouble is, you're underpaid and deserve a raise—now! You like the boss, and he or she likes you. But like many bosses, this one's tuned out: if you're gonna get a raise, you'll have to *ask* for it.

Do you have the picture? OK, go ask for your raise—in

your imagination. Put down this book, close your eyes, and walk into the boss's office. Go ahead, I'll wait . . .

Congratulations, you've just drafted a speech! And if you think about it for a moment, you'll recognize—perhaps to your delight—that it's an activity you've been engaging in all your life.

All of us walk around drafting little speeches in our heads: talks with the boss, chats with a spouse, talks with *anyone* where a little prior thought is required. That's what a speech is—a talk that's thought out in advance. But the best news is yet to come. The easiest way to *write* a speech—actually get it down on paper—is to follow the same imaginative process you just used in asking for your raise. Every good speech is *first* written in someone's head. *Then* it's transferred to a piece of paper.

Still sound difficult? It isn't. It's just like playing baseball: the rules are simple enough, but after hitting the ball, you do have to know to run to your right—toward first base.

Here's first base:

EVERYTHING MUST GO DOWN ON PAPER

You will never *ever* give a good speech if you don't first reduce *everything* to writing. That means every sentence, and every word of every sentence.

Now, don't jump to the conclusion that you're going to end up *reading* the thing to your audience. The final delivery may take place from notes, something we'll talk about later. But for now, your all-important starting point is a fully-written text.

Why? There are three reasons. You must have the *incentive* to think the speech through—word for word. You must have the *opportunity* to edit what you've started with. And you must have the *confidence* that comes only after you know that every word has been mapped out in advance.

Let's start with the last item, since it's the key to everything else.

All performers suffer from stage fright, to one degree or another. Some of the most famous names suffer the worst cases. That's understandable: when you're on top, there's always the remote chance that one horrible disaster will send you toppling to the bottom. To *insure* that it doesn't happen, there's constant rehearsal, constant practice. Every move, every expression, every syllable and note of music is repeated, over and over. Nothing is left to chance. That's how performers get themselves on stage—and why even the worst case of professional stage fright still isn't *paralyzing* stage fright.

I mentioned earlier that one thing I learned from Myron Cohen was that my colleagues and I were really in show business. Here's how that happened. Day after day, night after night, I listened to Myron telling the same stories. Funny stories, hilarious stories, stories that made me laugh each and every time, no matter how many times I had heard them before. And I began to notice that every word, every inflection, was always the same.

By contrast, the things my colleagues and I were doing would vary from function to function. Sometimes we received positive reactions from the audience, sometimes not. Why?

Myron provided the answer. We were winging it, and it showed. Oh yes, we had a good idea of the message we wanted to get across, but from performance to performance, our words were always a little different. Now, for the first time, I was able to see the importance of knowing how every *word* would work. Change a phrase here, or a thought there, and the *message* changes. Simple as that. When you want consistent, positive results, you must know where you're going every second.

And what's the result? Confidence!

STARTING YOUR DRAFT

You'll need a large pad of paper: a lined yellow legal pad is ideal, because it lets you spread out and launch trial balloons all over the place.

Begin *exactly* as you do in your head. Thank your introducer, greet your audience, and give them a general idea of what you're going to talk about. Go ahead and put it down, word for word. Use any abbreviations or shorthand you like, as long as you can read what you've written—not just today, but a few days from now. (You'll soon see why that's so important.)

In the beginning, you needn't worry about putting in the Six Signals. If they come naturally, and you may find they do, great. Otherwise, even if your talk is scheduled for tomorrow night, there's still plenty of time to stick them in.

Are you up to the point where you've announced the general theme? Good, now start a fresh sheet of paper. From now on, each item goes on a separate page.

Give the first point of your theme's development. For example, in your little "raise" speech, point one—*why* you deserve a raise—was probably the idea that you were doing a great job. Do the same thing here. Don't worry about getting each point in the right order—later on, you may want to move the "great job" argument to somewhere else in the speech. For the moment, just get it on paper—and once again, word for word.

Now move to another fresh page and write down thought-development number two. Avoid any concern that the thought isn't fully developed; just put down as much of it as occurs to you right now.

Another fresh page, and you're on to the third thought-development. "And furthermore. . ." Same rules as before.

At this point, you may begin running a little dry. If so, it's OK. Certainly more will occur to you later on—perhaps when you least expect it. On the other hand, if the old noggin is really banging away on all cylinders, just write a little faster. The idea is to get it *all* down, as soon as it occurs to you.

Ready to go for the big message? Put down your most important point ("I need a raise"). It may be just a sentence, and maybe that's all you need—simplicity sells. Or maybe you need several paragraphs; whatever it takes.

Do you have multiple-action points? ("I need at least ten dollars a week more.") New page, please. Would you like that raise to begin *this* week? Another page.

Now start wrapping up. (A lollipop for the boss, as a little extra incentive: "If I get my raise on Friday, I'll come in on Saturday and clean up the storeroom.") If you don't have a lollipop, don't worry about it: a perfect one may occur to you later on. Minds are wonderful things; you never know what's gonna pop—as in lollipop—out next.

Finally, your conclusion. (You want to thank your boss for his/her time, especially on such a busy day, and you look forward to getting a positive reply—soon.) ''And thank you very much.''

And that's it. You've done it! That's at least half of your preparation, and it's *on paper*. Now you're ready for step number two.

ADDING FURTHER DEVELOPMENT

Depending on how much lead time you have, you're going to find yourself adding further development to each section of the speech from time to time. From now on, no matter where you go—even if it's a trip to the supermarket—take along a notepad and a ballpoint pen. Halfway between avocados and celery, a new thought-development may suddenly occur to you. Jot down the thought right away. Then transfer it to the legal pad when you get home.

You'll find this sort of thing happening all over the place. Also, don't be surprised when you discover yourself mentally *giving* the speech as you walk along. That's very common—just watch the traffic.

If, on the other hand, you have only today to prepare your speech, take a walk. Right now! Take your pad and pen along. If it isn't safe to walk by yourself in your neighborhood, maybe you can just sit on the porch. Wherever; you want to be free, floating, and alone with your thoughts.

Start reviewing in your head what you've put on paper. Don't look unless you have to. If you find yourself rephrasing a particular thought, write it down that way—directly under the original version. Add sentences and thoughts whenever they occur to you, but don't delete *anything*. The idea is to accumulate as many choices as you can to express a particular thought—especially your main point.

THE FIRST EDIT

If you're starting to get nervous, that's OK, because it means you're starting to picture yourself up at the podium. But you're also starting to realize something else: that you're going to be the best-prepared person up there.

You'll need about an hour alone, at your desk or kitchen table. Try to silence all distractions. Take the phone off the hook. Send the kids off to a neighbor.

Begin by tearing all the used paper off the pad. Then do whatever it takes to get the thoughts they contain into some semblance of continuity. If a thought or phrase jotted down on the first page really belongs on the third page, cut it out with scissors and tape or staple it where it belongs—or on a fresh page, if need be. Shuffle and reshuffle until you're pretty sure you've got everything in the order you want it.

Now add whatever Signals are still missing. Use a pen with a different color of ink—so that the inserted Signals will stand out later. When you come to a sentence or phrase that's obviously wrong, change it or cross it out.

Even if things get really messy, don't worry as long as you can still read everything. Go through the entire speech, from beginning to end. Is everything there that's needed? Great, you're ready for some fresh paper.

Write out the entire talk from beginning to end, allowing triple spacing between lines. Don't worry about misspellings or punctuation, just write it all out. Number each new page in a large circle in the upper right-hand corner.

Next you'll need a pencil. Go back through your draft and underline the words you think you ought to emphasize during your delivery. If you need some guidelines on how to do this, just check through this book. Wherever I've wanted to emphasize a certain word or thought, I've used italics. Don't worry about choosing the wrong word—that's why you're using a pencil.

Now mark in your punctuation. Put *large* commas where needed to divide each thought into logical phrases. Again, you can use this book for guidance (although you may find yourself rearranging some of the marks later on). Finally, use two standard markings used by professional printers and proofreaders: place a small circle around every period, thusly. Underline the first letter of each new sentence three times.

Your edited draft is completed.

The First Reading

Immediately after the edited draft is finished, you'll want to read your speech aloud for the first time. (Continued privacy is important—you still need a good twenty minutes to yourself.) Take off your watch and put it on the table. Stand up. As soon as the minute hand hits the next five-minute designation, begin reading your speech in as loud a voice as you can—without causing yourself any undue embarrassment.

As soon as you're finished, look at your watch and mark the elapsed time on the upper left-hand corner of the top page. Don't worry if the talk ran longer than you expected: the first time through, it's normal for most people to read aloud at a slower-than-usual pace. Nor is there any cause for alarm if it's much a shorter than you expected. There's always plenty of room to add new material *if* it's really needed.

You'll most probably find that the thing is choppy—that it doesn't flow in a smooth, continuous rhythm. That's normal, too. You're making the transition from the written to the spoken word for the first time. Rearrange emphasis-words and commas where necessary, and insert longer pauses—by use of dashes just like the ones used here—if required. You should then read the speech aloud for a second time. Use your watch again, and mark the new timing under the old one on the top page.

THE EDIT-READING

Your speech is 90 percent complete. You want to give your brain a little breathing room, so go back to your normal activities for at least a full day.

At this point, a cassette recorder will come in handy. If you don't own one, perhaps you can borrow one. Set up everything at your work station, and, once again, obtain the necessary quiet and privacy.

The purpose of the edit-reading is to make the final transition from written to spoken grammar. You may have noticed that this book is written in a semi-conversational tone; that's my normal writing style, and it makes fairly heavy use of contractions (such as the word *that's* in this sentence). I think it's more fun to read because it avoids some of the heavy-handed formality present in straight, written English. The purpose of your edit-reading is to delete *all* of this formality and put your talk into a more relaxed, natural, conversational style.

Begin by searching your text for any word followed by the word *is. There is* should be changed to *there's, What is* to *what's,* and so on. Don't worry about overdoing it: it will look a lot stranger on paper than it will sound.

Now turn on the recorder. Stand up and begin delivering your speech. Don't worry about your timing—we'll come to that in just a second.

Once the newly-revised speech is on tape, play it back immediately. Listen for the points where you've placed your contractions, and see if they don't sound a lot smoother. You'll also notice places where they're still needed; in fact, they'll probably stand out in bold relief. *You will* will probably beg to be changed to *you'll, they are* to *they're,* and so on.

OK, you're almost at the finish line! Make all of these changes, and then record the speech once again—using the next blank spot on the tape. (Don't erase your first delivery.)

This time, your playback should sound almost perfect. Is a little additional informality still required in one or two spots? If so, touch 'em up and record one final version. Time the playback with your watch, and mark the time under the previous entries.

Finally, listen to the tape all the way through, from the first to the last recording. Do you hear yourself making vast improvements along the way? That's because you've adopted a more conversational style, and also because you're becoming better and better acquainted with the words themselves. You may even begin to hear something that *isn't* on the tape: the applause that's going to follow your final word. That's the audience, but it's also me. Well done!

We're ready to talk about your actual delivery.

Preparing the Delivery

Is your heart beating just a shade faster? Don't worry about it—it's normal, and happens to me all the time. You're just getting a lot closer to the actual delivery of your talk—which means that most of the work is done.

Most—but not all. At this point, you have a decision to make. You can deliver your speech as it currently exists—in full-text form—or you can convert it to the notes-only mode. Obviously, the choice is up to you. But if this is your very first time out of the gate, I strongly suggest that you stay right where you are. You're gaining a lot of confidence as you go along, but you may not be quite at the point where you want to tackle an informal presentation mode. In any event, read on—you never know when you might want to (or *have* to) give it a try.

CONVERTING TO NOTES-ONLY

Certain speaking situations require that the talk be given an informal treatment on its final delivery. The best example is the small meeting (usually 30 people or fewer) where everyone gathers around a conference table to discuss business. In this setting, a full-text delivery would be inappropriate: the speaker wants to talk *with* the audience, not *to* them.

Nevertheless, knowing *exactly* what you want to say is very important, especially where career advancement is at stake—as it sometimes is.

The other uses of notes-only delivery are for awards and presentations, building dedications, welcoming speeches, and outdoor ceremonies in general. Obviously, all regular talks and speeches can also be converted to this mode; we'll talk more about this later on. First, here's how to make the conversion:

You'll need a packet of 4-inch by 6-inch index cards (not the smaller 3-by-5 cards) and a red marking pen. If you're planning to give your talk from a seated position, you can type the cards using all capital letters, as shown on the upcoming sample card. If you'll be standing up or have poorer-than-normal vision, *print* your cards using large block letters and a black marking pen (the red pen is for underlining emphasis). The idea is to create "cue cards" indentical to the larger ones used by television personalities.

Begin by taking the full-text version of your speech and underlining the key words in each sentence that will help you remember the entire line. Here's the actual text of the talk that I used to introduce this book to the publisher's sales representatives:

[Following my introduction by Running Press publisher Lawrence Teacher:]

"Thank you, Larry, and good afternoon everyone. I know you book pros have heard every overblown adjective in existence, but The Overnight Guide to Public Speaking *is really a unique book—nothing like it is out there on the shelves at this moment. But before I give you a short tour of its contents, I need about a minute and a half to tell you about my background . . ."*

Now, here's the actual note card for that portion of the talk:

```
THANK LARRY -- GOOD AFTERNOON

KNOW BOOK PROS OBVL ADJEC -- BUT OVERNIGHT GUIDE

    UNIQUE -- NOTHING LIKE IT ON SHELVES.


BEFORE SHORT TOUR CONTENTS -- MINUTE & HALF

    TELL YOU MY BACKGROUND
```

As you can see, key words have been extracted from the text of each sentence and typed in capital letters. One crucial word—"UNIQUE"—has been underlined (in red, on the original card) for emphasis. Where a sentence must be continued onto the next line, it is double-spaced and indented. Otherwise, all complete sentences are triple-spaced apart, so that each can be quickly located.

As you can also see, each card is numbered in the upper right corner.

If you have written out your speech and edited it word for word, a short sit-down talk like this should require only one quick reference to each note card. Otherwise, you can talk directly to your audience, looking at various people from time to time, as befits an informal setting. The cards are, in effect, a safety net to provide you with confidence and quick reminders when needed. They are *not* a substitute for the draft stages of your preparation.

Which brings us back to the longer, stand-up speeches.

In the early 1960s, John F. Kennedy popularized impromptu speaking through the wit and charm of his famous press conferences. Interestingly, Kennedy's *speeches* were *very* carefully prepared, word for word. But what captured attention were the press conferences—with their frequent laughs—where the President spoke largely off the cuff.

Suddenly, everyone wanted to look like the handsome, charming man standing at the podium of the State Department auditorium (his favorite spot for meeting with the press). Prepared speeches were out; extemporaneous talks, *in*. And public-speaking teachers were happy to oblige.

Unfortunately for today's novice speaker, some speaking instructors still think that speeches can be prepared and delivered *only* from notes. This method is supposed to be very "with-it." In my opinion, it's also very stupid.

Most of us have very bad memories. With the vast amount of input we're forced to deal with every day, it's amazing that we remember our own phone numbers (some people don't, as you know). And a *ten-minute* talk consists of at least *a thousand* words. Nevertheless, some instructors (and books) insist that creating the actual text as you go along is the way to do it.

Perhaps, however, you are one of those fortunate people

with a superior memory. If you don't want to be tied to a full text (and as you'll see in a while, there *are* disadvantages to being tied), you can try committing your speech to memory, again using note cards as a safety net. Nevertheless, you should prepare from a complete, word-for-word text, exactly as outlined earlier. The advantage is that you're using the great memory trigger, the eye—and not just trying to "visualize the words" (whatever that means) in your mind, as some teachers would have you do.

Prepare the cards exactly as indicated earlier in this section. You'll simply need more of them. For this reason, I suggest a minimum of three rehearsals with your cassette recorder and *just* the cards. See how much you really do remember, and how it all sounds on playback. I also suggest you try a final rehearsal without *anything.* Take a long walk and see how much you remember when fully weaned from your support materials. This should smooth out any remaining rough edges.

Finally, I would suggest you take a fully-marked version of the text with you to the actual delivery, just in case. That's the step that's coming up next.

PREPARING YOUR FINAL TEXT

You're ready to prepare the final document you'll be using at the podium. Before you do this, though, remember one important fact: no one will ever see it but you. It can therefore contain any "personal" markings, codes, or other devices you need to assist your delivery.

Obviously, it is most important that this final text be *readable* from at least two feet away. If you must bend over to read each word, everything is for naught—you will lose all eye contact and intimacy with the audience, and your natural enthusiasm will be buried behind the podium.

If you do have fairly good eyesight, you can type the final copy on a standard machine. Use all capital letters, no lowercase, and the standard proofreader's marks (in red) of a triple underline under the first letter of each sentence and a circle around each period. This will help you find the location of each complete sentence very quickly—much faster, in fact, that with standard upper- and lowercase typing.

On the typewritten version, triple-space all lines, and allow generous white margins on each side. About 150 words to the page is right; any more, and you may be squeezing things in too tightly for easy legibility.

If you have weak eyesight, or just want to make sure you've got every last advantage going for you, consider renting a "bulletin" typewriter. (See the Yellow Pages under "Typewriters" for a nearby office-equipment supply house.) These are the machines used at conventions to type the names on delegate badges. They're clunky and cumbersome, but they provide marvelously readable final text for speeches. We've provided a sample that speaks for itself.

A BULLETIN TYPEWRITER CREATES LARGE-PRINT COPY, WHICH IS EASY TO READ AT A DISTANCE.

No matter what kind of typewriter you choose, the physical act of typing the copy yourself will greatly aid memory retention—even if you're a hunt-and-peck typist. I've seen people type the final versions of their speeches and then quote sentence after sentence without consulting the copy. Again, it's the eye-fed input to the brain that does it.

For the final typed version, use high-quality, rag-content bond paper if possible. This may sound like an extravagance— but it isn't. One thing most novices don't consider (until they're at the podium) is that when you're ready to move on to the next page, you must be able to get an *instant* grip on that piece of paper. Most rag-content papers are easily grasped by the fingers, but some cheaper papers are very slippery or stick together and can cause you a momentary fumble while trying to make the transition.

Incidentally, experienced speechmakers *never* turn the pages of a text—that's too obvious to the audience. The correct method is to grasp the top page and *slide* it to your left, thus exposing the next one, with minimal obvious effort. Nor do you care if the discarded page slips over or under the pages already completed—it's been read, and its job is over.

Of course, the final typed copy of your speech does *not* have to be letter-perfect: strikeovers, crossouts, and minor misspellings are all perfectly acceptable, as long as the thing is *readable.*

When you've completed the typing, proofread each page to make sure all words fall in their proper order and that you haven't made any unintentional deletions. Then, with your red marking pen, add the final touches. Underline the first letter of each sentence three times. Place a small circle around each period, and place a broad underline under each word to be given emphasis on delivery. Add any other codes you deem necessary. Finally, place a large number within a circle at the upper right-hand corner of each page.

It's done!

DIVIDE AND REMEMBER

The most famous speech in the history of our nation is certainly the Gettysburg Address.* It's also one of the shortest. Yet most adults can quote only the first thirty words or so, even if they were required to memorize the entire thing as students. How come? Because most of us think of it as a *single unit,* rather than as a number of smaller units—each of which could be remembered far more easily.

At this point, you're probably becoming very familiar with your own speech, particularly its opening portion. That's excellent: now, if you can remember just a bit more, you'll be well on your way to a first-class performance at the podium. The idea is to wean yourself away from the text. This provides increased opportunity for eye contact with the audience and, therefore, a far more enthusiastic and natural delivery.

The process itself is quite simple: just take a pencil and draw straight lines across each page of the text between the natural sections of your talk, thus dividing it into logical units.

Once you have done this, number each section (again in pencil) on the right-hand side, just under the dividing line. Now read it all through at least twice, beginning to end, paying particular attention to the beginning to end, paying particular attention to the *first words* of each section. Do *not* attempt to memorize the entire thing—that isn't necessary.

---

*It's a popular myth that Lincoln composed it on the back of an envelope on the way to the event: several drafts are known to have existed in the White House at least a week before the speech. Not even Lincoln would have dreamed of "winging" it!

Just concentrate on each opening phrase.

At this point, you'll want to make use of any thinking time you have available: driving to work (keep the radio off!), taking a shower, walking to the corner store, whatever. Try to review the speech in your mind. See if you can visualize where each line is drawn on the text and the words that immediately follow. If you do this on a regular basis, even if you have only a day or two available, you'll find yourself becoming ever more familiar with the *entire* text—no matter how bad your memory. When you spot a problem on a particular section, go back and re-read the text—but *only that portion*. Allow yourself to rely more and more on the retention process.

I've saved the best for last. Follow this procedure, and I absolutely guarantee that your confidence in yourself will improve a hundredfold. You'll find that emphasis-words now come automatically; that the entire shape and tone of your talk will make itself clear to you; that you'll actually *hear* yourself, up there at the podium, giving a happy, smooth, energetic performance.

And that's well worth the effort.

Preparing for the Podium

By this time, you're probably not only hearing yourself, but *seeing* yourself giving the talk. Perhaps what you see is a little frightening—because, once again, you're dealing with the fear of the unknown.

Not to worry! Once again, it's a simple matter of preparing for what's coming. And that's why you have this book; I'm still the tour guide pointing out the items of importance, and how to deal with them.

Recruiting an Accomplice

The accomplice system is one of the cornerstones of the method I teach, particularly for people giving longer speeches. It has its roots in one simple principle: never do alone what you can do much better with assistance.

The big problem with public speaking, particularly for the novice, is that you feel so very much alone—it's you against the audience. But it doesn't have to be that way. For the final stages of the project, simply find yourself a partner. Ask that person to perform a special—and highly rewarding—task: to become your *link* with the audience.

In my experience, the best accomplices are people who face public speaking tasks themselves: most often a colleague or a friend who's on a similar level of responsibility in a different field. I call this person an "accomplice" for one important reason: the activities involved are hidden from the audience. They fall into two distinct stages—before the speech, and during it.

Before your speech, the accomplice's job is to be your audience for one final rehearsal. Obtain some privacy, sit the person down in a chair (as far away as possible, so you can get the feel of "projecting") and give your talk from beginning to end, *without interruption.* If you happen to fumble somewhere along the line, just keep going: the idea is to give a *complete* performance. You can always do it over again if need be.

During this final run-through, have the accomplice pay particular attention to your pace and timing, giving you feedback on whether you're going too fast or too slow. One of the big virtues of involving the accomplice at this point (and not before) is that, just like your real audience, he or she is hearing the speech for the first time—and so will *not* know what to expect. That's exactly what you want: someone who will let you know if anything isn't totally understandable.

Also ask your accomplice to watch for any trailing-off of your voice at the end of sentences or phrases. Many people do this unconsciously—even in normal conversation—without realizing that they are depriving the listener of a crucial element to total understanding. In the English language, the end of the sentence usually contains a key word or phrase that modifies or explains the balance of the thought. When this crucial component is misunderstood—or goes unheard—the listener can easily misconstrue the entire thought. For example, if I mumble the final word of, "I'll see you at eight tomorrow evening," the listener could easily think I mean tomorrow *morning!* Obviously, such a misunderstanding can cause both embarrassment to the speaker and anger on the part of the listener; and this holds doubly true in the meeting room. If your accomplice hears any instance where you're guilty of trailing-off, give this aspect of your delivery some extra special attention.

Finally, you'll want your accomplice to listen to the *emotional* tone of your delivery. The thorough manner in which you've prepared your speech should already be paying a bonus in the form of much greater enthusiasm for the project, and you want to be certain that this feeling will be projected to the audience. If a little additional work is required in this area, it's well worth it: when the message is delivered with zest and conviction, audiences always respond in kind.

Using your accomplice to critique each of these areas in advance provides yet another "safety net," and one no speaker should be without.

During the actual talk, the accomplice stands at the very back of the room, but in the speaker's line of sight. If the podium is at stage right (the right side of the platform as you face the audience), then the accomplice's position is toward your left, at the rear of the room. From this position, the accomplice communicates with the speaker through four distinct hand signals:

A *flat hand*, facing and raised toward the ceiling, means, "Increase your volume—you're talking too softly."

A *single finger at the mouth* means the traditional, "Softer, you're a little too loud."

A *circular motion with the hand* means, "Speed it up, it's too slow."

And a *stretching movement with both hands* (like pulling on a very large rubber band) means, "Slow it down, you're talking too fast."

Practice these signals in advance so that both of you become accustomed to what they look like.

The benefits of the accomplice system are obvious. In addition to making it a "team effort," the accomplice provides the otherwise missing link that tells you what you cannot always know yourself: *how* you're doing, *while* you're doing it!

Try it. You may decide never to face another public speaking task alone. And don't forget—when your partner's turn comes up, *you're* the accomplice.

HANDLING VISUALS

I have mixed feelings about talks that employ slides or other visual elements. On the one hand, they can be very effective in presenting complex materials—and help the audience understand through visual reinforcement what cannot be explained with words alone. On the other hand, visuals are almost always cumbersome, slowing the pace of the presentation far below what's required for complete audience involvement. There's another drawback, too: when it comes to visual presentations, most audiences are highly sophisticated. Just think of all the fancy tricks they're doing on news and sports telecasts these days, and you'll see how really' boring a simple slide show can be to the average audience.

When visuals are needed, my advice is to recruit *two* accomplices. The regular one signals you and also performs the important function of adjusting the lights. (Nothing looks less professional than asking someone in the audience to do this for you, and waiting while that person hunts all over for the control box.) The second accomplice runs your audiovisual device. One full rehearsal should take place so that everyone knows the order of presentation, which slide falls where during the talk, and what the *final* slide looks like.

Most people who present visuals fail to bear in mind one important fact: they are *not* members of the audience. Whereas the audience needs to study and absorb the visual data, the speaker doesn't. Yet many speakers continually look at the screen while talking. That's a big mistake. You're talking to the audience, so face *them*. You already know what's on the slide; it's not going to inform *you* of anything.

I suspect that many speakers who face the screen simply haven't prepared their remarks properly and are relying on the slides to prompt the words they're going to say. That's big mistake number two. Having visuals in your presentation doesn't relieve you of the responsibility of preparation and rehearsal—if anything, it's the other way around.

Do everything mentioned in this book so far, and in *addition*, mark your final text with the *exact* instant at which each slide is to appear. (Also mark the "lights off" and "lights on" cue points in the text.) Then make two photocopies, and give one to each of your accomplices. That's *really* professional: it builds all the necessary signals into the script and presents the audience with a polished performance.

In a mixed audio-visual presentation, advance preparation of *everything* is the key. Leave *nothing* to chance! Take along extra bulbs, extension cords (you never know where the outlets will be), and anything else you think might be needed. Do it all, and you'll be head and shoulders above the crowd—and well on your way to an excellent presentation.

LOOK YOUR BEST— FEEL YOUR BEST

It's time to give some thought to your wardrobe and other personal grooming considerations. Do you need a haircut—or are you thinking of changing the style a bit? Now's the time to make that appointment—but *not* for the day of the talk. With your luck, your regular hair stylist will be out that day, with no adequate substitute available. Arrange it at least a day or two in advance.

If you're a woman and depend on makeup to any degree, you might want to find out exactly what type of lighting will be present in the room. The fluorescent fixtures in some meeting facilities can change the color rendition of makeup from what you see under standard incandescent light.

Your most important consideration, however, is what you'll be wearing. Perhaps you have something nifty all picked out, or have decided to buy a new outfit. Either way, you should have a complete understanding of what you want to accomplish.

Audiences want you to look a little special—just enough so that it's clear you went to the effort, but not so much that you'll look out of place (wearing a tux in the afternoon, for example). Again, it's a matter of validating the audience's decision to come to the event. When you obviously care about how you look to them, it makes them feel good about you, and *themselves.*

That factor is frequently ignored by many experienced speakers who should know better. Once again, you can learn from Myron Cohen, as I did. Just as we were about to get started on the first evening of our first tour, I looked around the headtable to find Myron's chair empty. My tablemate informed me that he was upstairs changing into his "stand-up" suit. I was puzzled: just a bit earlier, Myron had been sitting there in a coat and tie like the rest of us, and he'd looked fine to me.

When his introduction was at hand (I was doing the honors), I looked offstage to see Myron standing ready in the wings, and spiffy in a superb blue suit. The jacket fit like a glove, and his trousers had creases such as I'd never seen before—standing out like elongated razor blades along the front of each pant leg. This, he later informed me, was one of several suits he'd had made especially for his banquet performances. While wearing one of these "stand-up" suits, he never permitted himself to sit down: if he did, the special sewn-in creases and other features would be ruined. Five minutes after every performance, Myron was back in his room again, changing into a normal suit.

That's show biz, but also a fine example for the rest of us. Myron *looked* great and gave a great performance, and I'm convinced the two were linked together. Even a professional needs the lift that comes only when you know that *every* single thing is working in your favor.

GESTURES

I deliberately haven't spoken about gestures until now because, frankly, I *wanted* you to forget about them. Nevertheless, they're probably on your mind. Almost every first-time speaker has the same urgent question: just what *do* I do with my hands?

Here's the simple answer: whatever comes naturally. Would you like a great seminar on hands and gestures? You can attend one that lasts only thirty seconds and will tell you everything you need to know. If you own one of the newer video recorders, just tape any Johnny Carson monologue and play it back in the "fast-scan" mode. You'll see his hands flying all over the place: behind his back, grasped in front, waving, pointing, at his belt, at his face, you name it.

That's the name of the game when it comes to gestures: you name it! If it's appropriate, allow yourself to do it. And don't worry about how it looks. The audience will simply absorb your gestures as part of the entire package of words and movement—you being you. That's exactly what you should want.

STAGE FRIGHT AND NERVOUS ENERGY

We talked earlier about stage fright being very common among professional performers. It's really the body preparing itself for a big event, just as it does for your first downhill run on skis or your first time at the wheel of a car. Everyone gets it, and everyone gets it *differently*. Yours may be just a little queasy feeling in the stomach, or a slight sensation of weakness at the back of the knees. Sweaty palms are fairly common. Many people go a little dry in the mouth (tip: drink a little extra fluid during the preceding three or four hours). Mine usually comes in the form of suddenly feeling very cold, particularly around the shoulders.

Whatever form it takes, it's normal; and for some people, it's actually exhilarating. In any case, stage fright is *not* your big problem. Your big problem is nervous energy, because *that* shows. And if you let it get out of hand, it can seriously detract from your performance. You have probably seen this happen dozens of times: the speaker whose fingers drum constantly on the side of the lectern, or who shifts body weight from one foot to the other, back and forth, back and forth. One of the worst forms is the person who twiddles with eyeglasses—that can make audiences *very* unhappy.

Go into a toy store and buy a kid's rubber ball that's large enough to cover most of your palm. On the morning of your talk, start walking around with the rubber ball in your hand, squeezing it vigorously all the time. Now shift it to your other hand and do the same thing. Now back again. Keep it with you constantly until it's time to leave for the function. Then put it away. Its job is done.

From then on, the minute you feel the nervous energy start to mount, just think of the rubber ball. Curl your fingers around it and give it a good mental squeeze. That'll do the trick. I don't know why; but it works for me, and it works for anyone I've ever taught it to.

A final word about alcohol and tranquilizers: these items are *not* in your best interests, and you must avoid them, no matter how keen the temptation. If you eat in moderation on the day of your talk—as I've suggested several times earlier—a big glass of water will do you more good than any form of pills or booze. Just remind yourself that being nervous is as natural as sleeping at night. I'd worry if I *didn't* feel that way; and in fact, many actors say that the time to worry is when you *don't* feel nervous just before you go on. A performer needs that extra kick of adrenaline to be at his or her absolute best.

Just be good to your body, and it will serve you very well when the big moment comes. Then when it's over, you can reward it in any way you see fit.

HEADTABLES, PODIUMS AND OTHER BARRIERS

In business, there's no more effective barrier to good communication than your office desk. Sit behind it, and you're vested with all the authority of a Persian king. And who wants to talk to you honestly when you look like that?

The same general problem applies to headtables, podiums, and the other devices speakers use. As long as you're behind that *thing*, it acts as a barrier between you and the audience.

At least podiums are usually necessary: they support your written speech and usually have a built-in light for better visibility of your text. And several new models make an attempt at solving the barrier problem by using see-through bottoms that give the audience an idea of what you look like from the chest down. Nevertheless, I always find some way to slip out from behind the thing for at least a few seconds. I know audiences pick up good vibes from this, and I urge you to try it yourself.

Unfortunately, you can't slip out from behind a headtable. These absolutely useless objects are monuments to the vanity of the human race. OK, you have a bunch of distinguished guests and people who have worked hard for the group. Does that mean we have to look at them the *whole* time—while they're eating, drinking, chewing the fat—and most particularly, while some poor individual is trying to communicate with us from behind the thing?

To their credit, some meeting planners now see the problem with headtables and are attempting a variety of solutions. The most obvious is just to do away with the stupid contraption, but most organizations won't stand for that.

The next best solution is to place the podium *somewhere else:* off to the side or in another section of the room. If you find yourself presented with such an arrangement, find whoever did it, and give 'em a big hug! That person knows the problems of speakers and has solved one of the biggest of them all: having to compete with other people at the headtable for the audience's attention.

Microphones

Most modern podiums come equipped with a removable microphone on an adjustable base. You should *not* have to bend over in order to be heard. If the volume isn't properly adjusted, have the situation corrected. (That's another reason you should always arrive early for your talk.)

I have very mixed feelings about the lavalier type of

microphone, which strings around the neck or is clipped to your tie or blouse. On the one hand, it permits freedom of movement and lets you step away from the podium for a few seconds now and then—not a bad idea, as you now know. On the other hand, the little devils can work themselves out of position. And you may be unaware that the microphone has stopped picking up your voice until your accomplice or someone in the audience (usually rather pointedly) calls it to your attention. Five minutes later, the thing could be out of whack again. And yes, there's also the danger of tripping over the cord—I've seen lots of folks do that.

DISTRACTIONS

Be prepared for anything! I've seen just about every distraction known to the human race, and still, every now and then, along comes a new one. While one of my seminars was in session, a guy came into the hotel ballroom to replace some burned-out light bulbs in the ceiling. If I hadn't put a stop to it, I'd have had eighty-five people staring up at the chandeliers for the next half hour.

Distractions just go with the territory. The cardinal rule is that if you can't avoid being interrupted, just *stop.* If a waiter drops a tray, the audience is going to watch the dishes being picked up. You may as well remain silent and save your breath. In a few moments, the audience will turn back to you automatically. (After all, how fascinating can broken crockery be?) And *then* you can proceed. Just give 'em a wry smile, as if to say, "What can you do?" They'll understand.

THE BIG DAY

Plan to get there at least thirty minutes before the audience starts assembling. Go up to the podium, test the microphone (if it isn't on already, get someone to turn it on). Go to wherever you'll be seated, sit down, then get up again and walk to the podium. Do this *at least* four times. You want to get the complete feel of the walk.

Now go out to where the audience will be seated and sit down. Get up and move to another chair. Go to the back of the room and sit down again. Get the complete feel of the hall.

Back to the podium again, and one more time through the up-and-down routine. There's applied psychology at work here, as I've explained before. The idea is to make it *your* podium. You're the insider now; it's your audience who will be the strangers.

This whole process should take no more than ten minutes. Then pack up and take a brisk walk—around the block, if you can. Do this, and I guarantee that whatever stage fright you have when the audience *does* arrive will be minimal—and controllable. The room is simply part of your equipment; you're borrowing it for a little while so that you can do the job you set out to do. It's quite simple, really—because it's the truth!

THE ART OF
INTRODUCING—AND
BEING INTRODUCED

Your introduction is *your* responsibility. Just handing someone your resume will *not* do the trick. Anyway, who really cares where you went to school and how many kids you have?

The purpose of an introduction is not to boost your ego, but to prepare the audience for your speech. It should be short, punchy, and *very* to the point. Put yourself in the audience's shoes: what would *you* like to hear? Answer that one, and you're on your way.

First, the audience wants to know the area of your expertise and *why* you're qualified to speak to them. Give them the reason, short but sweet. You specialize in . . . , or

you're associated with . . . , or you've won an award for . . . .
That information goes first.

Next, if appropriate, the audience will want to know about
you as a human being. But not a list of all your clubs and
activities. Most of the people out there in the seats do those
things, too. Isn't there something unusual about your life—
perhaps a hobby or sport that's a bit out of the ordinary? People like to know about those things—and they mark you as
a well-rounded individual who'd be a worthwhile friend.

Finally, they want to know who you are—your name, pronounced correctly. Mine's tricky: it's pronounced, "Wall-
Mith." If yours is Adams, don't worry about it. Otherwise,
spell it out *phonetically* for your introducer. When someone
fumbles your name or says to the audience, "I *think* this is
the way it's said," the people in the seats will wonder how
worthwhile a guest you really are. That, as you now know,
is the way audiences think.

All of which means that your last job is to type out your
introduction, word for word. Triple-space it, exactly as you
did your text, and, before giving it to your introducer (at least
several days in advance), make at least four copies. You never
know when you'll need one again; and an extra copy must
go with you to the affair: people do get sick at the last
moment, and you may find yourself being introduced by
someone rushed in at the last second—and who doesn't have
your intro because it's at home with the person who's ill.

But if luck is with you, you'll get the person originally
scheduled to do the job. A very smart move on your' part
would be to invite that individual to lunch, about a week in
advance. Have your introduction ready at that time. Not only
does this give the person extra rehearsal time (which is very
much in *your* interest), but the introducer will also get to

know you as a person, allowing a little ad-libbing at the podium, which good introducers love to do. Thus things can be said about you that you wouldn't dare put on that piece of paper for fear the introducer will tell everyone you wrote it yourself. (And tell they will, particularly if the person's a regular member of the organization.)

Here's a typical introduction. You can spot the ad-lib quite easily:

> *Our featured speaker tonight comes from the world of motion pictures—but not the part that's visible to audiences, except on the list of credits that follows the 'end title' of each film. In fact, very few of us know anything about the aspect of movie production that takes place before the cameras roll: Who are the people walking on the street behind the main action? Is the street vendor a professional actor, or just someone who happened to be available at the time? These decisions are the province of the casting director, and tonight we have a veteran of the business with us to explain all about it. He's won numerous industry awards for his work and is involved in the production of two major features to be released this fall. Incidentally, he's also a fine actor and has appeared in supporting roles in over seventy films—a fact he doesn't normally tell about himself. I know you'll find his talk fascinating. It's my great pleasure to introduce Mr. Cecil Pound-worthy . . .*

Notice two things about this introduction: while the general area of the speaker's expertise is revealed, the specific topic of the talk is not. In most cases, mentioning the title of the speech lends an unnecessary formality to the introduction—which should be spirited and breezy. In any event, the opening few seconds of the speech itself should give the audience all the information it needs.

Notice too that, in good show business style, the introduction does not mention the speaker's name until the very end. That's the "Applause" sign, just like the one in the TV studio.

Applause is the goal—the target you should aim for when writing your introduction, or in giving one for someone else. It's the launching pad, the blast-off, the booster rocket that every speaker needs.

And when your applause comes—as it will—I know you'll rise smartly from your chair, walk briskly to the podium, and flash those pearly whites as you thank your introducer for being so gracious. Then let 'em have it . . .

I'll be out there rootin' for ya!

Talk Show
Appearances

Even though they involve a different *type* of talk, radio and TV appearances are as much a part of modern public speaking as speechmaking itself. And, not surprisingly, many of the rules of the road are exactly the same. It's the *responsibility* that's different: the talk show host* is *required* to make you follow the rules, whether you want to or not.

A good talk show host will not let *anyone* waste the audience's time or be disorganized to fail to provide the proper credentials. Sometimes these goals are achieved by subtle methods that neither the guest nor the audience may be aware of at the time. (And as indicated earlier, pre-screening and interviewing by the production staff play a large role.)

---

*Contrary to popular opinion, this word has no gender. It can be male or female—just like the talk-show hosts themselves.

But when these "gentle nudges" aren't working, the host has no choice other than direct action—which some guests wrongly interpret as rudeness. It isn't, it's simply the host doing his or her job: to keep the audience both informed and entertained. Remember, the host will be there—with that same audience—long after you've departed; and your segment must keep the audience alert and involved no less than any other.

This fact doesn't relieve *you* of the job of preparation—far from it. If anything, preparing for a talk show requires more advance work than preparing for a formal speech. In the banquet hall, *you* maintain control over what the audience hears and when they hear it; in a talk show appearance, it's the *host* who maintains control.

The schedule of commercials is the single most important factor in determining how this control must be applied (except, of course, on public TV and radio). Thus, if a host has exactly four minutes until the next commercial break, the guest cannot be permitted to take the discussion into a new area that will obviously leave the audience bewildered if it isn't explained at some length. What area *will* the host explore to fill that four-minute slot? You don't know. You must be prepared for anything.

The good guest knows the topic area backward and forward, and can spring with light-footed agility from one subtopic to another. That takes preparation—a thorough review of the subject, with particular attention to recent events and developments. Has a hot, new discovery just been made? Ask the producer or talent coordinator why you're being invited at this time, and then do everything you can to update your knowledge.

Many of the other questions you will want answered in

advance are identical to things you would want to know in a formal speaking situation. Who are the other guests? How much time is being allotted to the subject? How much does the audience (and the host!) already know about your topic area? Was it covered in another recent broadcast? If so, who were the guests at that time, and what was said? Perhaps a transcript or recording of the earlier show is available.

Talk show hosts are the same as the rest of us; they have their opinions and biases, some of which are more evident than others. The prospective guest may not be able to discern exactly what they are; but you can certainly determine the overall *tone* of any show from past performance. Do your homework: watch or listen to as many of the daily broadcasts as you can. If you can't be at home, take a small radio or TV to the office—or set up a video or cassette recorder to tape the show for later review.

Take notes on everything you hear and/or see. Use your watch to time typical segments that are likely to be the same length as yours. Pay close attention to how the host approaches the topic: is it in a general way at first, with more specific questions following later? Or does this host jump right into the thicket with immediate questions of a pointed nature? See if you can juxtapose your topic with what is being discussed on the earlier broadcast: if you just had those couple of seconds to reply, how would *you* handle the question?

In short, use the show itself as your preparation guide and seminar. If something's being done on a regular basis, it's being done for a *reason*—usually because that's what the host and producers have found is most effective with that particular audience.

As with everything in public speaking, that's the final key.

Talk shows revolve around the *collective* interests, knowledge, and ego of the particular audience involved. Find out everything you can about that audience, and you're well on your way. Ask the show's producers. *They* know—and they'll respect you all the more for asking in advance.

How to Profit When You're a Captive in the Audience

Make life a continuing seminar on public speaking. There are always things you can learn from others. Whenever you're at a speaking function, carry a small notepad. It gives you the opportunity to spend your time profitably, no matter *what's* going on.

In particular, take detailed notes whenever you detect something that isn't as it should be. Is the speaker losing the audience? Why? What mistakes in delivery and content are being made? Which of the Six Signals are missing?

Observe the audience around you. What do they react most favorably to—and most negatively? Write it down.

Observe everything around you: the room, the lights, the platform setup. Is anything beyond the speaker's control contributing to the problem? If so, how might you deal with it in the same situation?

Finally, ask yourself this question: Have I learned anything today that will help when *I'm* the speaker? If the answer's "yes," you've made a very smart investment in your future.

A Speaker's Bookshelf

Need a lollipop? Here's a starter set of great reference sources for anecdotes, quotes, unusual facts, and other handy information—plus a nifty book to help you with pronunciations of difficult words.

A Browser's Dictionary [1980]
By John Ciardi
Hardcover: Harper & Row
The phrase, "bury the hatchet," has its origins in an American Indian ceremony. The teddy bear was named in honor of Theodore Roosevelt. Explanations of these and thousands of other words, phrases, and expressions can be found in this fascinating book.

The Dictionary of Misinformation [1975]
More Misinformation [1980]
By Tom Burnam
Paperbacks: Ballantine Books

Before you tell your audience that Fulton invented the steamboat, or that Columbus proved to a disbelieving world that the earth was round, better check these books. Neither statement is true! Two great paperbacks, loaded with lollipops.

Fascinating Facts [1977]
By David Louis
Paperback: Ridge Press/Crown Publishers

A treasure trove of unusual facts. Stalin's pipe was a phony—he smoked it for effect, and only at public appearances. Christopher Columbus was a blond. Wyoming was the first state to give women the vote. Vintage port wine takes 40 years to reach maturity. All this and much, much more, all arranged by subject.

Guinness Book of World Records [Revised annually]
By Norris McWhirter
Paperback: Bantam Books

A combination of *both* useful and useless data—but always great fun. Although *Guinness* is one of the most popular books ever printed, it's doubtful that anyone actually reads it from cover to cover—which makes it all the more nifty when you quote one of the zillions of records to your audience.

The New York Times *Everyday Reader's Dictionary of Misunderstood, Misused, Mispronounced Words* [1972]
Edited by Laurence Urdang
Hardcover: Quadrangle/New York Times Book Company

A speaker's bible of correct pronunciations and usages of thousands of difficult (and interesting) words. If you'd like to know how to say *rhetoric* as opposed to *rhetorical* (they're pronounced differently), this is the book to have.

Nobody Said It Better [1980]
By Miriam Ringo
Hardcover: Rand McNally & Co.

If you'd like to tell your audience what one famous person said about another (Roosevelt on Churchill: "Winston has a hundred ideas a day, of which four are good."), or what a well-known personality had to say about himself (James R. Hoffa: "I sometimes make mistakes, but I am never wrong."), here's where to find 'em. *Triple* indexed: by subject, author (or editor), and key words. Highly recommended!

The Oxford Book of American Literary Anecdotes [1981]
Edited by Donald Hall
Hardcover: Oxford University Press

Fascinating lollipops about—and from—some of the best American writers of the present and past: Hemingway, Fitzgerald, Steinbeck, Thoreau, to name just a few. Even if you don't use one of these stories in your speech, observing the way they're *told* is worth the price of admission.

INDEX